D1103967

MINNESOTA PIONEERS

Acknowledgements

Credit is gratefully given to Miss Rosella Trawicky, Principal of Douglas School in Minneapolis. To Mrs. Martha Bray and Miss Betty Engebretson, Minnesota Room, Minneapolis Public Library. To the Minnesota Historical Society, St. Paul, Minn. To Mr. Joseph Zalusky, Hennepin County Historical Society, Minneapolis, Minn. To Mrs. Kenneth Johnson, Minneapolis, Minn. To all others who assisted me in gathering information for this book.

Minnesota Pioneers

Word Pictures of Famous Characters and Interesting Events in the Story of Minnesota.

by Mabel Otis Robison

Publishers

T. S. DENISON & COMPANY

Minneapolis

The Foreword

This is a book about men and women who helped to build the State of Minnesota. One of its purposes is to show that even the earliest explorers and those who followed were often professional people of learning who gave up wealth and comfort to use their training to make Minnesota, so blessed by nature, the illustrious State it has become. These character sketches follow in a sequence that depicts the development of the State in logical order.

It is also the purpose of this book to show the history, government, economics, and resources of the Territory and State through the lives of the characters, since no commonwealth can become greater than its people.

Maps accompany most of the character sketches so that students may trace movements and events. By studying each map as it appears, the child should have a complete knowledge of the colorful geography of the State when the book is finished. In a few instances where maps are not shown, the locations mentioned will have been previously shown.

It is hoped that the word pictures and photographs of these famous characters and interesting events will make Minnesota come alive in the minds of its children.

Mabel Otis Robison.

Contents

CHAPTER ONE—Pierre Radisson and M. Grosseiliers
Adventurers 7

CHAPTER TWO—Father Louis Hennepin
French Explorer, Missionary 11

CHAPTER THREE—Daniel Du Luth
Trader, Peacemaker 14

CHAPTER FOUR—Le Sueur
Trader, Miner 18

CHAPTER FIVE—Jonathan Carver
The Explorer 20

CHAPTER SIX—Captain Zebulon Pike
Government Explorer, Surveyor,
Astronomer 24

CHAPTER SEVEN—Joseph Renville
Fur Trader, Guide, Interpreter 28

CHAPTER EIGHT—Major Lawrence Taliaferro
Indian Agent 30

CHAPTER NINE—Philander Prescott
Interpreter, Superintendent of
Indian Farming 33

CHAPTER TEN—Joseph Renshaw Brown
Speculator, Politician, Inventor 35

CHAPTER ELEVEN—Colonel Josiah Snelling
Commandant 40

CHAPTER TWELVE—Pond Brothers
Missionaries 45

CHAPTER THIRTEEN—Major Stephen H. Long
Topographical Engineer 49

CHAPTER FOURTEEN—Henry Schoolcraft
Geologist, Mineralogist 51

CHAPTER FIFTEEN—Pierre Bottineau
Guide, Voyageur, Interpreter 54

CHAPTER SIXTEEN—Henry Hastings Sibley
Trader, Politician, Military Man 57

CHAPTER SEVENTEEN—Rev. Doctor Williamson
Missionary 60

CHAPTER EIGHTEEN—George Catlin
Artist, Explorer 62

CHAPTER NINETEEN—Joseph Nicolas Nicollet
Astronomer, Geologist, Cartographer ... 65

CHAPTER TWENTY—Martin McLeod
Trader, Politician 69

CHAPTER TWENTY-ONE—Franklin Steele
Realtor, Lumberman, Capitalist 72

CHAPTER TWENTY-TWO—Anson Northrup
Builder, River Man 75

CHAPTER TWENTY-THREE—Henry Rice
Politician 77

CHAPTER TWENTY-FOUR—Father Lucian Galtier
Missionary 79

CHAPTER TWENTY-FIVE—Norman W. Kittson
Fur Trader, Legislator 81

CHAPTER TWENTY-SIX—Paul Bunyan
Legendary Logger 84

CHAPTER TWENTY-SEVEN—Harriet Bishop
First Public Schoolteacher 87

CHAPTER TWENTY-EIGHT—Alexander Ramsey
First Governor 89

CHAPTER TWENTY-NINE—Edward Duffield Neill
Preacher, Educator 99

CHAPTER THIRTY—James Henry Goodhue
Editor 102

CHAPTER THIRTY-ONE—Little Crow
Indian Chief 104

CHAPTER THIRTY-TWO—Colonel John H. Stevens
Father of Minneapolis 106

CHAPTER THIRTY-THREE—Joe Rolette
Fur Trader, Legislator 110

CHAPTER THIRTY-FOUR—Charles Eugene Flandreau
Indian Agent, Jurist, Soldier 112

CHAPTER THIRTY-FIVE—Loren Collins
Soldier, Jurist 115

CHAPTER THIRTY-SIX—The Mayo Doctors
Surgeons 118

CHAPTER THIRTY-SEVEN—James J. Hill
Empire Builder 121

CHAPTER THIRTY-EIGHT—Jane Gray Swisshelm
Editor, Abolitionist, Lecturer 124

CHAPTER THIRTY-NINE—William D. Washburn
Statesman, Businessman 126

CHAPTER FORTY—Ignatius Donnelly
Orator, Politician, Author 128

CHAPTER FORTY-ONE—John S. Pillsbury
Father of University, Statesman 130

CHAPTER FORTY-TWO—Henry P. Whipple
Bishop 134

CHAPTER FORTY-THREE—Thomas B. Walker
Lumberman, Patron of the Arts 136

CHAPTER FORTY-FOUR—Merritt Brothers
Miners 139

CHAPTER FORTY-FIVE—John Ireland
Archbishop 142

CHAPTER ONE

Pierre Radisson
and
Medard Grosseiliers

Adventurers

The Pilgrims had lived on our shores about twenty years when young Pierre Radisson and his brother-in-law, Medard Grosseiliers, entered the territory which is now Minnesota. They came down from Canada to Prairie du Chien, then paddled up the Mississippi River.

Along the Mississippi River. — Bluffs towered along the western shores. They passed wooded islands, separated by patches of water lilies and hyacinths. Small streams rippled into the Mississippi River through stretches of black walnuts on the hillsides and black maples in the swamplands. On the summits of the bluffs, the men saw stunted white cedars. On the eastern slopes, blue grapes grew almost to the water's edge.

They stopped at a place now called Winona to camp where red mulberries grew among slender birches. At the top of a high bluff they saw a signal fire. They knew some Indian brave

Radisson and Groseilliers among Indians

7

They saw trees along the bluffs.

was up there, sending warnings ahead of their coming, wondering if they were friends or enemies.

At Prairie Island. — They passed through Sioux hunting grounds, seeking ducks in sloughs and pockets, throwing stones at gobbling, wild turkeys, and catching bass and sunfish. They came to a beautiful place in the river which they named Prairie Island. There were buffalo and deer on the island, and the river was full of fish. Today Hastings and Red Wing are nearby.

For more than a year they tarried there. They made friends with the Indians. Young Radisson joined them in their hunts. He went with them to get berries, wild rice, and maple sugar. It was easy for him to follow the ways of the Indians because, as a boy, he had been captured by a band of Iroquois in Canada. He had lived with them for a full year before he escaped.

Even in winter he went with his Indian friends, hunting and fishing through the ice. They fashioned snowshoes to their feet to get over the drifts.

Groseilliers collects furs. — While Pierre roamed the country with his Indian friends, Groseilliers remained at Prairie Island, gathering corn and supplies for their trip back to Canada, and collecting furs. He wanted to show the French officials in Canada the great possibilities of building up a trade with those Indians. He persuaded five hundred Indians to return to Canada with him. He wanted them to enter into an alliance with the French government, which then controlled Canada.

8

First trading expedition from Minnesota. — They canoed and portaged their way to Montreal. Then they gathered into a brigade of fifty bright-painted canoes. Loaded with furs and Indians, the canoes sped down the St. Lawrence River to Quebec. This was the first trading expedition from Minnesota and very effective it was. Citizens of Quebec gathered along the banks to see the brigade come in. They examined the rich furs and listened to stories of the fabulous wilderness. Traders came down to make offers for the furs. Radisson and Groseilliers were feted as heroes. The Canadian officials were so impressed they made trading agreements with the Indians from Minnesota.

Radisson and Groseilliers return.— Radisson and Groseilliers wanted so much to return to Minnesota that they came back without getting a permit from the Governor of Canada. Because of this they were simply adventurers and not emissaries of the Canadian Government.

This time they went to a point on the south shore of Lake Superior where they built a log cabin, facing the vast waters. The savages there, never having seen them before, were suspicious and hostile. The two men pretended they had been sent by the Great Father. Wishing to impress the savages, Radisson tossed powder into a small fire. When it flared up, the Indians were sure it was magic. They decided the white men must have great powers. After that they treated them with more respect, inviting them to their games and dances.

A scene on a Northern Minnesota Lake

They canoed and portaged to Montreal

9

The big famine. — There was a terrible famine that winter. The Indians hibernated in their scattered villages. The two white men were left alone in the little cabin by the cold waters of Lake Superior. The snow fell so deeply they could not get out to hunt. They resorted to eating old, ground-up bones. They stripped bark from trees and cooked it. They dug under the snow and found moss to cook. They even made soup from old beaver skins. As Radisson went out one day to get wood, he fell through some ice. He almost froze his feet before he could get back to the cabin. He was lame all the rest of the winter and suffered great pain.

The spring meeting.—Spring came at last. Twenty - four Sioux called with gifts of fish and other food. The men were so glad to see them they spent eight days in feasting. Other bands joined them. They challenged each other to athletic feats. They sang and danced and exchanged gifts.

When the meet was over, Radisson and Groseilliers crossed to Mille Lacs. Out of Mille Lacs they followed the Rum River to the Mississippi River. There they met some Ojibways on a trading expedition. They went north with them by way of the St. Croix River. This circular trip took two months.

They return to Montreal. — Crossing the west end of Lake Superior, they visited the Cree tribe near the future site of Two Harbors. This time they persuaded about three hundred Indians to return with furs. Again they swept into Montreal with great noise and display.

However, the Governor of Canada was displeased. He said they had no business going on such a mission, pretending they were exploring for Canada, when they had no permit. He fined them both heavily and confiscated the furs.

The Hudson's Bay Trading Company started. — Remembering how they had suffered through the long winter, the two men became very angry at such treatment. As a result they went to England and influenced a group of wealthy men to establish the Hudson's Bay Trading Company. Later this company become so powerful it controlled most of the fur trade for many years.

The records they left.—The Pigeon River, a part of the northern boundary of Minnesota, was called Groseilliers River on French maps for a long time. Radisson and Groseilliers seem to have been the first to leave written records of their explorations, and those records are very colorful.

Pigeon River was called Groseilliers on many French maps.

CHAPTER TWO

Father Louis Hennepin

French Explorer Missionary

Father Louis Hennepin was very happy that year of 1681 when he was transferred from France to the New World. He thought the Mississippi River led to the Pacific Ocean, and he was eager to explore it, acting as missionary to the Indians at the same time.

He came with the La Salle expedition to explore the Mississippi. When the expedition reached the great river, La Salle sent Hennepin north; then he himself went south. Before they parted, La Salle furnished Father Hennepin with 2 knives, 12 awls, and some beads, needles, and tobacco as gifts for the Indians. He also gave him a calumet peace pipe. There were two other men with Father Hennepin when they started up the Mississippi River in a small canoe, catching turtles and fish for food as they went.

Father Hennepin captured.—They had reached only the future site of Winona when they met a fierce looking war party. The war party surrounded them, ready to kill them. Father Hennepin held out the peace pipe. The chief took the pipe away from him. Then he took all the gifts which La Salle had given Father Hennepin to take along. The Indians stopped to quarrel over the tobacco. None of them tried to take his chalice because it glistened so in the sun that they thought it might be magic. They insisted that the white men come along with them.

They canoed north to the present city of St. Paul. Father Hennepin managed to keep his compass and tried to figure out directions. As soon as he took it out, all the Indians gathered around in great curiosity. They gave Father Hennepin the name of "Black Blanket" because of his robes.

At Mille Lacs.—When they reached St. Paul, they left the canoes and started to walk north. At the Rum River they had to swim across, though there was still ice in the water. They waded dirty swamps and climbed hills so thick with bushes that Father Hennepin's legs were cut and bleeding. Once he dropped down on some dry grass to rest. The Indians set fire to the grass to make him go on. Finally they reached Mille Lacs where they had a tent settlement.

Father Hennepin was so weak he thought he would surely die, but a kind squaw gave him steam baths and rubbed him with wildcat grease. They took away his priestly robes and gave him a hobe of beaver skins, trimmed with beads and quills. One of the chiefs used his black robe to carry the bones of dead men on his back.

Father Hennepin

Father Hennepin kept praying for delivery. Whenever he prayed, the Indians got angry, thinking he was trying to turn Manitou against them. He had an iron pot for cooking, to which he had clung the whole time. The Indians would not touch this because it had feet like a lion's claws.

His work in captivity.—One of the chiefs adopted him as a son. Afterwards things were easier for him, though the Indians never let him forget he was their captive. He, in turn, never forgot he was a priest, and he tried to help them whenever he could. He made a little dictionary of Indian words. He showed the Indians how to plant seeds and raise a crop. He cared for the sick children. His captors began to trust him.

12

They waded through swamps

Father Hennepin names St. Anthony Falls.

He names St. Anthony Falls. —

During the summer they took him along on a buffalo hunt. Roaming south, they came to some falls that made a noise like thunder. Father Hennepin was amazed at the sight of the tumbling water with little green islands at its base. The islands were crowned with trees, overhung with grapes and ivy. All about them the water curled and roared.

He called them the Falls of St. Anthony, and they are still known by the same name, though their appearance has greatly changed. On a tree he engraved a cross and the arms of France. He was probably the first white man to stand there.

As the hunting party returned by way of the Rum River, Father Hennepin carved his name on a stone where Anoka now stands. They worked their way back to Mille Lacs. This time Hennepin did not get so tired as he had previously because he had become accustomed to life in the woods.

Today the name of Hennepin is given to a county as well as to a Minneapolis street. The Father Hennepin Memorial Highway Wayside, on the southeast corner of Mille Lacs, marks the spot where he was held captive.

If you would like to know how he got away from his captors, read the story of Daniel Du Luth which follows.

CHAPTER THREE

Daniel Du Luth

Trader . . . Peacemaker

The city of Duluth on Lake Superior is a memorial to a young nobleman who took his life in his hands to make peace with the tribes of Minnesota.

Daniel Du Luth was a French lad who went to Montreal in Canada in search of adventure. While he was in Montreal, which was then a fur-trading city, he listened to the tales of the voyageurs when they came in with their furs. He longed to become one of them. However, he had to return to France to join the Royal Service as required of young men at that time.

Du Luth meets Hennepin. — The chaplain of his regiment was a young priest named Father Hennepin. Father Hennepin was just as curious

about the new country as was Du Luth. They talked a great deal about it, and Father Hennepin asked many questions about Du Luth's stay in Montreal.

Du Luth returns to Montreal.—As soon as his army service was over, Du Luth returned to Montreal. He was a dashing figure in his curly black wig and fine satin and brocade clothing. He had a certain charm that made him at home in any social circle. Renting a house in Montreal, he bought furs from the river-men and listened to more stories of the wilderness.

Goes into the wilderness.—Suddenly two tribes in what is now Minnesota began a big war against each other, both tribes wanting the rich hunting land. They could not get furs and fight at the same time, so trade fell off. Du Luth decided he would go into the wilderness to see if he could make peace between the tribes.

Some other young Frenchmen who also were looking for adventure decided to join him. They went to the Sault which is part of Michigan and gained the friendship of the Chippewas. Du Luth convinced the Chippewas they would benefit by trading with the French in Canada. He did not try to influence them by giving them liquor as so many others

Bear

ndian Camp.

did. Using honest friendship, he established a trading post and told the Indians he would buy all the furs they brought there.

Meets the Indians. — From the Sault the Frenchmen followed Lake Superior through its snarling waters to its western extremity. There were bears and other wild animals in the woods. The country was alive with danger, but it was beautiful too. Indian wigwams stood along the point which is now Duluth. Canoes rode in the water. Tall pines and hardwoods grew right to the edge of the water. The area was called Fond du Lac, meaning "End of the Lake." There Du Luth called a Council of Indians and raised the French flag on the shores of Lake Superior.

Finding the Indians did not harm them, the explorers made their way through the dense woods to Mille Lacs. Standing on the shore of the

15

big sparkling lake with the squalid Indian village behind them, they were surrounded with dark, sullen faces. They acted as if they were unafraid, and through an interpreter they talked a long time with the suspicious red men. They found that the Indians thought Mille Lacs was inhabited by ghosts that sighed and moaned in the night.

Talking the savages into good humor, Du Luth planted the French flag. The tribes recognized that Du Luth had a power so strong it could break down inter-racial barriers and superstitions.

Father Hennepin freed. — During further conversation with the Indians,

They rode the sparkling lake.

Along the St. Croix.

16

Du Luth learned that a priest was being held captive by a tribe at the south end of the lake. Immediately he started after the tribe and caught up with the captors two days later. Imagine his surprise when he found the captive to be Father Hennepin, who had been his chaplain back in France. The two men embraced, happy to meet again. Hennepin related how he had been adopted by the chief with six wives and had lived mostly on wild rice and smoked fish.

Du Luth informed the Indians that Father Hennepin was his brother and they must let him go. They did let him go but they followed the Frenchmen to the Sioux village on Mille Lacs where a council was held. Finally Du Luth persuaded them they should let him take Father Hennepin back to Canada.

Father Hennepin went down the Rum River to the Mississippi until he reached the Wisconsin River. He went up that river and portaged through dense underbrush across Green Bay and up into Canada.

Further explorations. — The next year Du Luth returned to explore the St. Croix River from Lake Superior to the Mississippi River. This route became a much used thoroughfare by Indians, explorers, and missionaries.

It was almost two hundred years before a city grew up at the point of the lake where this man stopped, but the city was named Duluth in his honor.

Deer

Indians on the lake.

17

Duluth grew up at the point of the lake

CHAPTER FOUR

Le Sueur
Trader . . . Miner

A famous canning town in Minnesota bears the name of Le Sueur, although it is about 250 years since Le Sueur came to Minnesota. Having heard the stories of Radisson and Groseilliers and of Du Luth and Father Hennepin, Le Sueur also wanted to visit this astonishing country. He entered the Sioux territory in 1694 and established a post on Prairie Island in the Mississippi River at the end of Lake Pepin. This was the same island where Radisson and Groseilliers had wintered more than forty years before.

Le Sueur and his men hunted all fall and found plenty of game. As soon as it got cold, they hung the game on scaffolds to preserve it through the winter.

LeSueur takes the Indians to Canada.—In the spring savages came to Le Sueur's post to sell furs. Then, passing the future site of St. Paul, he took the Indians up to Montreal to see Governor Frontenac, who was their "Great Captain." The Indians were much impressed when Frontenac gave them an audience. The chief of the Ojibway band from La Pointe made a speech, begging that Le Sueur be sent back to them. A Dakota chief then spoke. He laid out a beaver robe and placed 22 arrows on it. He explained that was the number of villages that desired Frontenac's protection through Le Sueur.

Le Sueur goes to France—Count Frontenac promised to send Le Sueur back and to give them protection.

However, Le Sueur did not go back to Minnesota with the red men. Instead, he went to France to get a license to open some mines about which he had heard through the Indians. They had told him the mines had blue and green earth which the Dakotas dug from the rocky bluff of the Blue Earth River near the present site of Mankato. The Indians used the earth as a paint, but Le Sueur felt sure it was copper.

A fort at the mines.—Because of various difficulties, Le Sueur did not get back for almost five years. Then he came up the Mississippi River from New Orleans. He and his companions saw rattlesnakes from four to six feet long. They made wooden whistles to call the elks so they could shoot them for food. They reached the Blue River where the mines lay. Le Sueur camped there, hoping to learn more about them and to trade for beaver furs at the same time.

He and his men made a fort which they named L'Huillier. Part of the men stayed at the fort while the others hunted buffalo. That winter they lived almost entirely on buffalo meat, eating about six pounds a day. In the spring they went to work at the mines. They were able to scratch out the mineral with knives. They filled three canoes and added some curious stones they had uncovered.

Le Sueur returns to France.—That spring, Le Sueur took 3600 beaver skins from the Indians in exchange for tobacco, knives, and bullets. He

Indian Chief.

loaded the skins in canoes. With the mineral and the furs he went down to New Orleans, leaving twelve men to hold the fort.

When Le Sueur got to New Orleans, he met D Iberville, the governor of Louisiana, who was his cousin by marriage. They took the green earth and the pelts back to the king of France. The earth proved to be worthless, but the pelts were valuable.

Le Sueur deserves much credit for increasing geographical knowledge and influencing the Indians to better relations with the whites.

Sioux Encampment.

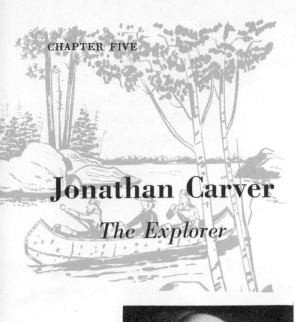

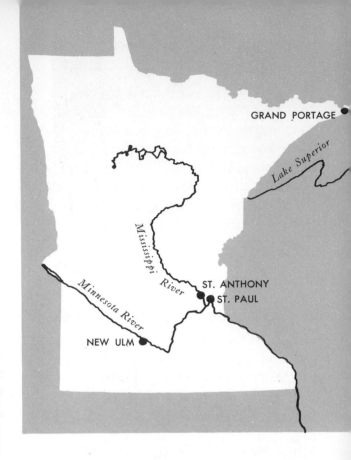

CHAPTER FIVE

Jonathan Carver

The Explorer

Though Jonathan Carver was from the Eastern part of what is now the United States, the country still belonged to Great Britain when he came to explore in Minnesota before the Revolutionary War. This exploration was almost a century after Du Luth rescued Father Hennepin. Because Minnesota was then under the British flag, there was freer trade with the Indians, and a number of traders had palisaded forts on Minnesota rivers and lakes.

Up the Mississippi River.—It was the year 1766 when Jonathan Carver came up the Mississippi River with two companions in a canoe. They stopped to camp near the mouth of the Whitewater where they found artificial mounds on the ledges. They passed up the river where the white bluffs were heavy with dark hardwood and then went through the bluff-walled, 34-mile lake in the Mississippi River called Lake Pepin.

Views the Falls of St. Anthony.—Winter had set in when they reached St. Anthony Falls, and Carver made a sketch of the Falls clothed in ice and snow. This sketch was later made into an engraving. He declared he had never seen such a beautiful country and was sure that palaces would some day replace the Indian huts.

arver's Cave.

Explores the Minnesota River. — With the British flag floating at the head of his canoe, he went up the Minnesota River, which was then called St. Peters. He spent the winter with a band of Indians where New Ulm was later to be laid out as a German settlement. In the spring the Indians migrated to the locality of fu-

ture St. Paul which was then wild country. They brought along some of their dead to be buried in the Indian mounds at the top of the bluff overlooking the river. These mounds are still in evidence, and as you stand there today, you may look down on trains, boats, and airplanes, all evidence of how transportation has grown since then.

The Indians' service in a big cave.— The Indians carried the most important dead man, a chief, up a steep, winding path to a white sandstone cave in the side of what is now known as Dayton's Bluff. Placing the body in a sitting position on a mat, they put eagle feathers in his hair and beaded moccasins on his feet. Then they held an elaborate ceremony, chanting and dancing and wailing. During the rites, the braves pierced their arms with arrows and the women gashed their legs until the blood ran.

ndian Mounds.

St. Anthony Falls.

When he looked about the cave, Carver could see that there were many moss - covered hieroglyphics left by Indian visitors. Back in the darkness of the cave was a very deep pool of water. He remained with the Indians until the ceremony was completed; then he accompanied them to the top of the bluff where the body of the chief was buried in one of the mounds.

The next day they all returned to the cave to hold a council. At this council Carver made a speech. He told them that the king of England across the waters was their Great Father. The Indians listened with deep interest. They were so impressed to think he represented the Great Father that they made him a chief of their tribe. They also ceded him a large piece of valuable property, but this claim was never recognized by the Federal Government. The Indians remained at the mounds for some time, securing food by hunting and fishing.

Carver at St. Anthony Falls.—Carver returned to the Falls at St. Anthony, accompanied by the chief of the Winnebagos. They looked at the beautiful sight of a rainbow above the water, formed by the sun hitting the spray. The chief thought the Great Spirit lived at the Falls. Wanting to make him an offering, he threw his pipe into the stream, then his tobacco roll. He took the bracelets from his arms, the rings from his ears, and the ornaments from his neck and cast them on the waters. He tossed his arms about, praying that the Great Spirit would give them protection. Since he had tossed away his pipe and tobacco, he insisted that Carver should light his pipe so they could smoke together in honor of the Great Spirit. Carver complied; but he also measured the Falls, estimated their capacity, took their geographical position, and speculated on their future value. Though a wilderness of more than a thousand miles lay between the Falls and the New England settlements, Carver felt sure that Minnesota would attract travelers.

He hunts for a northwest passage. —He thought, like so many others thought, there was a northwest passage across the continent. With this belief he went up the St. Croix River and across Lake Superior to Grand Portage the next summer. He talked to many of the traders from distant posts who came to Grand Portage from the interior, but none of them knew of such a passage.

Returning home, he tried to get someone interested in building a fort at Lake Pepin as a center of future exploration. The first stirrings of the Revolutionary War were brewing, and no one could give attention to a small fort in the middle of a great wilderness; so nothing came of his efforts at the time. Carver had to be content with writing an account of his travels, and the book became a best seller.

Along the St. Croix.

23

CHAPTER SIX

Captain Zebulon Pike

Government Explorer
Surveyor . . . Astronomer

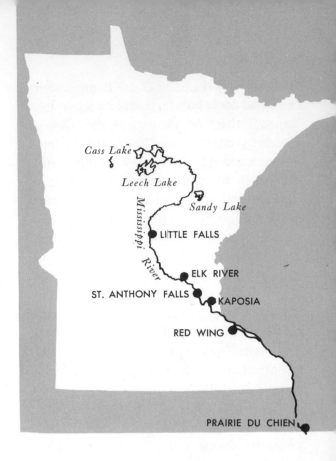

Interest in the upper Mississippi River increased after the Louisiana Purchase. Zebulon Pike was appointed by President Jefferson to make a survey trip to that part of the new territory which was Minnesota. He was instructed to record everything about the land, find out the size of the Indian population and where the Indians lived, make alliances with them and tell them they now belonged to the United States, expel the remaining British traders, look for places that might be suitable for military posts, and see if he could find the real source of the Mississippi River. As President Jefferson knew about St. Anthony Falls, he suggested that it might be a good place for a military post.

Zebulon Pike starts for Minnesota. —At that time Zebulon Pike was a second lieutenant 27 years old. He had been in service since he was about fifteen years of age. Pleased with his assignment, he left St. Louis in a seventy-foot keel-boat with several men and supplies for four months including food. A month later they reached Prairie du Chien, an outpost on the frontier where a few traders lived.

At Prairie du Chien he left the keel-boat and took two bateaux because he thought they would be easier to handle. He passed a village of Dakota Indians ruled by Chief Kupahasha, who carried a swan's wing, dyed scarlet. The Indian tent village later became known as Red Wing.

Pike Island.—About two weeks later Zebulon and his men reached the mouth of the Minnesota River. They camped on an island which still bears Pike's name. They had no sooner landed to cook a meal than 150 warriors came to see if they had any gifts for them. Pike made a speech, telling them the President of the United States was now their Father. After they had listened, he gave them small gifts. He hired a certain Joseph Renville to guide his party on and act as interpreter. He liked Renville very much. He knew a poor interpreter could turn the Indians against them.

In fact, he liked Renville so much he recommended him as a government interpreter.

The site for Fort Snelling. — Following the Mississippi River under Renville's guidance, they reached the bluffs of St. Paul-to-be. There was the Indian village of Kaposia, under the leadership of Little Crow, grandfather of the Little Crow who later

Pike's Island

25

Zebulon Pike travels north in Minnesota.

led the Indian massacres. Grandfather Little Crow was a good man. He made a treaty with Pike, selling him land along the river for a fort which would some day be Fort Snelling. The land extended as far as St. Anthony Falls which Father Hennepin had named almost two centuries before.

Promises to the Indians.—Pike explained to Little Crow that the government would establish factories at the post so Indians could buy supplies cheaper. He told the Indians the government would pay them $2000.00 for the land. He also made a deal for the government to buy a piece of land at the point where the St. Croix flows into the Mississippi River, because he believed that this might be a good spot for a fort.

Surveys to the north.—Pike and his men proceeded up the Mississippi

river. At one place they saw so many elk they named it Elk River. Pike surveyed all the way, noting the geology of each region, studying the stars to get their bearings. He never retired at night until he had copied all his notes for the day.

On reaching Little Falls, they erected two blockhouses for men and provisions. They called the place "Painted Rock."

Zebulan Pike Plaque.

Winter was at hand and Pike had not yet reached the source of the Mississippi River. At the blockhouses he and his men built sleds and made snowshoes. Then they struggled through snow and cold to reach Sandy Lake where a trader lived in comparative comfort.

He had a stockade a hundred feet square. Bastions were pierced for small arms. Pickets thirteen feet high surrounded the post. On entering the main gate, Pike saw first the residence of the trader with another large building nearby for voyageurs. On the western side there was a large store, a workshop, and a residence for the clerks. The trader had horses, raised potatoes, and caught plenty of fish and game. He bought wild rice and maple sugar from the Indians. Pike spent almost two weeks at Sandy Lake and his men built more sleds so they could go on.

Seeks the source of Mississippi River. — Leaving Sandy Lake, they went by way of Willow River to Pokegama Falls and then followed the Mississippi River to Leech Lake. Here they found another establishment with a main building, sixty by twenty-five feet, in which the director lived. Pike ordered that the flagstaff, which was fifty feet high, fly the United States flag. The trader complied with Pike's wishes. Pike found many of the Indians had small British flags which had been given to them as gifts. These he confiscated.

He was loath to leave the comfort

Little Crow Village.

of the Trading Company, but he forced himself to go on to Cass Lake, thinking that it must surely be the source of the Mississippi River. The weather was so cold and the blizzards were so bad, he could not explore Cass Lake as he wanted to. He returned to Leech Lake to hold a council with the Indians. He told them they must no longer pay allegiance to the British since they were now Americans.

He returns to Washington.—Satisfied that he had carried out his mission to the best of his ability, he went down the Mississippi River and returned to Washington. He gave a full report of everything he had done. He urged the government to push exploration in beautiful Minnesota.

The government was worried about the approaching War of 1812. Sailors were being impressed and ports blocked by the British. However, Pike was sent west on another trip with Fremont, and Pike's Peak marks the place he went.

When he returned home, he was drawn into the War of 1812 and died a soldier's death in Canada.

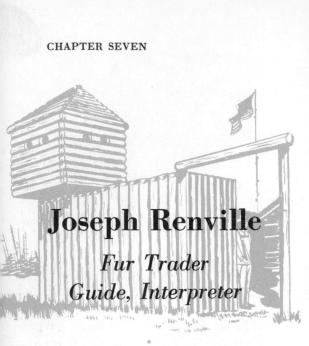

CHAPTER SEVEN

Joseph Renville

Fur Trader
Guide, Interpreter

LAC QUI PARLE

MENDOTA

Minnesota River

If you have ever been at Renville, you will enjoy reading about Joseph Renville for whom the town was named.

He was born near St. Paul in 1779, the son of a French trader and a Sioux mother, connected with the Kaposia band that lived near the present city of St. Paul. His history formed a link between the past and the time in which he lived.

A guide and interpreter. — While still a young boy, his father sent him to Canada to study French and the elements of the Catholic faith. After returning to Minnesota, he became a coureur de bois or river-man. You have already read about how he guided Lieutenant Pike from Prairie du

Chien to the trading post at Mendota when Pike came to explore Minnesota. He took Pike also to the Falls of St. Anthony. Lieutenant Pike liked Renville so much that he recommended him to the government as an interpreter. Renville acted in this capacity for several years and later, acted as a guide for Long's expedition.

Renville opens a trading post.—Mr. Renville entered the service of the American Fur Company under John Jacob Astor. In this job, he moved to Lac qui Parle where he built a trading post. Around the post he built a stockade which he called Fort Renville.

With an Indian girl for a wife, he lived like a baron. His estate was surrounded by voyageurs, Indian relatives, and half-breeds. There was a large tepee camp outside the stockade for his private army of Sioux warriors. He taught the wild Indians to plant corn which was the first seed corn planted in that part of Minnesota. He accumulated large herds of cows, horses, and sheep.

People on the road as explorers or traders always tried to stop at his post when night came, as they could be sure of a warm welcome and good food.

Annual Trip to Mendota.—Once a year Renville took a big brigade carrying furs to Mendota, and brought back supplies for the coming year. He always stopped for a visit with his friend, Henry Sibley, who was another baron of fur-land.

Renville joins the Mission Church. —In 1835 a mission under Reverend T. S. Williamson and Reverend Riggs was established at Lac qui Parle. Renville, who owned one of the first Bibles in Minnesota and hired a clerk to read it to him, encouraged the Indians to accept the religion of the white man. He helped to translate the Scriptures and hymn books into Sioux so the Indians could get the messages better. He spoke the Sioux language fluently and could translate from the French or English when it was read to him.

He loses his wealth.—Mr. Renville died a poor man because he was so generous with all who asked his help. He supported such a large retinue

Spearing Fish.

Renville's carts

of followers that when the fur trade slackened after the Treaty at Traverse des Sioux, his wealth declined.

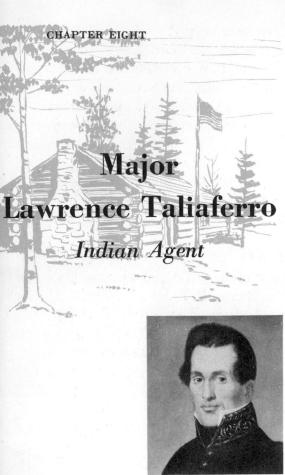

CHAPTER EIGHT

Major Lawrence Taliaferro

Indian Agent

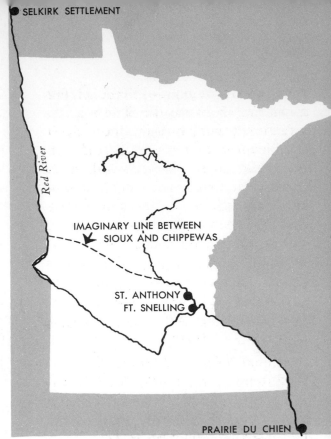

SELKIRK SETTLEMENT

Red River

IMAGINARY LINE BETWEEN SIOUX AND CHIPPEWAS

ST. ANTHONY
FT. SNELLING

PRAIRIE DU CHIEN

Where Fort Snelling now stands, there was practically a wilderness that summer of 1819 when 25-year-old Lawrence Taliaferro came to work as Indian Agent. The place was called St. Peter's. His job was to look after the Indians, keep peace between the Sioux and the Chippewas, and protect the fur trade. He had received a rating as major in the War of 1812.

The Council House. — Near his house was a big Council House built of logs where he could hold meetings with the tribes. He got the Sioux and the Chippewas to come there and smoke calumets together; but these meetings did little good since the two tribes fought every time they met in the forest.

His slaves.—He brought with him several black slaves. The Indians called them "Black Frenchmen." Taliaferro had a servant girl named Harriet Robinson who was later married to Dred Scott at Fort Snelling. Dred Scott was a slave of the Fort Surgeon, Doctor Emerson. By reading history, you will find out about the Dred Scott case which created such a stir years later in St. Louis when Dred Scott sued for his freedom because he had once lived on the free soil of Minnesota. Many think this case hastened the Civil War.

An honest trader. — Some of the traders in Minnesota tried to sell the Indians liquor so they could cheat them out of their furs. Taliaferro would not permit this villainy if he found out about it, and no trader could do business without a license from Taliaferro. He was an honest man and expected honesty from others, doing everything he could to protect the Indians from the greed of unscrupulous men. Both traders and politicians soon learned they could not influence Taliaferro to do wrong.

Fort Snelling established. — Shortly after Taliaferro came, Fort Snelling was established and a new era began for Minnesota. Navigation, farming and exploration fanned out from the Fort. When the sawmill was erected at St. Anthony to make lumber for the fort, Taliaferro often went down to watch the building and he commented that the mill was being well built.

Trade was opened with the Selkirk settlement on the Red River. At the same time problems with the Indians increased. Taliaferro was always truthful with them and appreciated their fondness for clothes, ceremony, and oratory. He realized that such things made them feel important.

Takes Indian representatives to Washington. — In 1824 he took Indian representatives from both the Sioux and the Chippewa tribes to Washington to show them the power of their White Father and to get them to join other tribes in friendly relations. Little Crow from Kaposia went along, and while he was in Washington, someone gave him a double-barreled gun which he carried everywhere. Henry Sibley was present to represent the fur trade. Since Sibley had served as a delegate to Congress, he knew how to get to see important people. It was agreed in Washington that the tribes should hold a mammoth

Indians on the river

Chippewa Chief.

conference as soon as they returned. This would be held to settle all their difficulties.

The big council at Prairie du Chien. —The big council did come about the next year at Fort Crawford near Prairie du Chien. Hundreds of Sioux and Chippewas came. Agent Schoolcraft from Michigan brought down 150 Salteaux. They came, escorted by soldiers bearing banners and playing musical instruments. Their boats swept down the river with flags flying, drums beating, and guns firing. They pulled up at the levee in an imposing array.

The dividing line.—The Sioux and the Chippewas drew up a dividing line which passed from Fergus Falls, west of Alexandria, to cross the Mississippi River between Sauk Rapids and St. Cloud. Each nation agreed not to cross this imaginary line except for peaceful purposes. They failed to keep this agreement. Three years later Sioux Indians killed some of the Chippewas within sound of Fort Snelling.

He establishes a farm school. — Major Taliaferro established the first farm school in Minnesota at Lake Calhoun in 1829. The purpose of this school was to teach the Indian boys to make a living through agriculture. He believed the missionaries should promote the use of the plow and hoe along with the Bible. As missionaries came, they did help him in this idea. Almost every missionary school maintained a farm to teach the Indians to till the soil.

In 1832, Major Taliaferro brought a wife to the Agency. She was a talented musician and their home became a social center. They lived there twenty years, and during that time Major Taliaferro exercised a wise influence over the tribes.

Chippewa camp.

CHAPTER NINE

Philander Prescott

Interpreter
Superintendent of Indian Farming

Philander Prescott came to Fort Snelling in 1819 as a clerk for the sutler. At that time most of the people around the Fort lived on the natural products of the land. Following the example of the Indians, they ate wild sweet potatoes, wild beans, wild rice and prairie turnips. The wild turnips were often dried and ground into flour.

Philander Prescott was put in charge of an experimental farm near Lake Calhoun because Major Taliaferro wanted the Indians to learn how to farm. Philander also did trading with the Indians.

Prescott buys a wife.—One of the Indian chiefs owed Philander a debt and gave his daughter, Mary, in payment. They had several children and Prescott had even taken to farming

on a claim near Lake Calhoun when he decided he was tired of having an Indian wife. He left them and went South where he wandered from one State to another. One night he went to a camp meeting and was converted. He decided then that he must go home, find Mary, and take care of her and the children.

Returns to Minnesota.—Returning to Minnesota, he found that Mary and the children had gone on a hunting trip with her people. They had gone clear into the Dakotas after buffalo. He packed some provisions in a sack and started on foot to find them. It was a long, hard walk and he asked Indians he met along the way if they had seen the hunting party. At last, after weeks of searching, he found them. The children were happy to see their father and Mary was glad too. Philander took them all back to Minnesota. He went to the missionary, Samuel Pond, and they were married in the white man's way.

He was a roamer in spite of his family. In 1834, he took up some land at Traverse des Sioux. He became sick there and gave it up. Three years later he had a claim at a point on the St. Croix River where Prescott is now located. There was trouble about that claim and he had to divide it with another man. Finally he went back to Fort Snelling to work as an interpreter and the family lived in a log house nearby. Almost every traveler who came that way was entertained at Prescott's. His oldest daughter grew to womanhood and he sent her to a Mission School to be educated.

Wedding at Prescott's. — When Prescott's daughter returned from Mission School, she fell in love with a man named Eli Pettijohn who worked around the Fort and Mission grounds. Eli was a big white man who made the floor shake when he walked across it. He talked in a booming voice. He asked Philander's daughter to marry him.

Philander arranged an elaborate wedding for his daughter. Officers from the Fort came in full dress uniforms with their ladies in evening clothes. Bois Brules were there, and relatives of the bride in blankets. Guests came from St. Paul and St. Anthony. It was a wedding that went down in history.

Some time later Philander and his son-in-law built a flour mill at the mouth of Minnehaha stream and it prospered.

Indians kill Prescott.—A very sad thing happened to Philander Prescott. He had been moved to Lac qui Parle to serve as an interpreter. One day he was told he must flee for his life since the Indians were massacring all the white people. Knowing his Indian wife and children would be safe, he jumped on a horse and fled towards safety. On the way some Indians shot him. He is buried beside his wife in Minneapolis.

Prescott's home in Minneapolis during his prosperous days

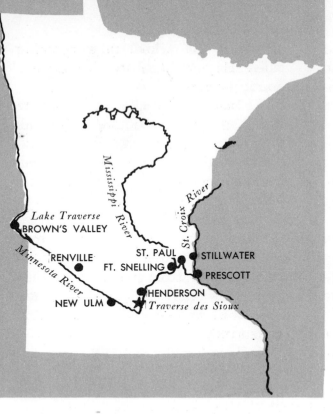

CHAPTER TEN

Joseph Renshaw Brown

Speculator . . . Politician
Inventor

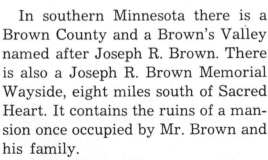

In southern Minnesota there is a Brown County and a Brown's Valley named after Joseph R. Brown. There is also a Joseph R. Brown Memorial Wayside, eight miles south of Sacred Heart. It contains the ruins of a mansion once occupied by Mr. Brown and his family.

Always first.—He came to Minnesota in 1819 when he was only fourteen years old as a drummer boy at Fort Snelling. He sounded the first reveille in Minnesota and helped to lay the first cornerstone in the fort at Snelling.

When he was seventeen, he and Colonel Snelling's son followed Minnehaha Creek to Lake Minnetonka, making that lake known for the first time.

He received permission from the Colonel to break up a piece of ground near Minnehaha Falls just to prove he could raise a crop there. He raised grain and cut a lot of hay.

By the time he was twenty, he was a sergeant under Colonel Snelling. Faithfully he attended the Sunday School class organized for young adults under Mrs. Snelling.

Soon after, he left the military

35

service and people all over the territory began to hear the name of Joseph R. Brown. Everywhere men went they could laughingly say, "Joe Brown was here." He seemed able to think ahead and be first in everything.

A good example of this was when Franklin Steele went to St. Croix to stake out a claim for water rights. He expected to be the first one there, but across the river he saw Joseph R. Brown cutting logs and trading with the Indians. Brown managed also to float his logs down the river ahead of Steele.

He was on a trading expedition clear across the state near Lake Traverse the next year when he got into some trouble with the Indians. They killed his team and would not let him take out some furs he had accumulated. Joseph Brown appealed to Mr. Renville's Trading post for help and Mr. Renville sent his son to the rescue.

On the St. Croix.—Next year Joe Brown was back in the St. Croix Valley, running a trading post on an island, sixteen miles from St. Paul. He had also been elected to serve as justice of the peace. The first trial by jury was held before him, and a strange trial it was. Philander Prescott, who served as an interpreter around Fort Snelling, had taken a claim at the mouth of the St. Croix River. Another man jumped it and Prescott brought the case before Justice Brown.

A jury was picked and it was decided the entire jury should go down and look at the claim which was forty miles away. They started in canoes but there was ice in the water and they had to leave the canoes and walk the last half of the way. They looked over the claim and started back to hold the trial. Returning to the canoes they found they had been burned so they had to walk all the way home. When they finally reached Marine and the case was held, the jury disagreed. As a result, Justice Brown advised the two men to divide the claim which they did.

Wisconsin legislator. — Shortly after, Mr. Brown was elected to serve in the Wisconsin legislature, since he was in what was then Wisconsin territory. There he learned a lot about parliamentary law and how to influence men. When the county was organized, Joseph Brown's claim became a part of Stillwater, which helped to make him a wealthy man.

No man's land.—In 1848, Wisconsin was admitted to the Union and the boundary lines were drawn in such a way that the St. Croix valley east of the Mississippi was not included and became a sort of no-man's-land. Joseph Brown decided it should be a part of Minnesota. He called a convention at Stillwater, getting the help of Franklin Steele, Sibley and others. They nominated Sibley to preside, but Brown made most of the motions and he suggested the new terri-

Log jam in St. Croix River.

tory be called Minnesota with St. Paul as the capital.

Sibley told them he had planned to spend the winter in Washington and if they would make a resolution, naming him as a Representative, he would use his authority to urge that Minnesota be admitted to the Union as a Territory. They passed the resolution and he went to Washington to get a seat in the House of Representatives. He got Minnesota admitted as a Territory with the area between the St. Croix and Mississippi Rivers as a part of the Territory.

Member of Minnesota Territorial Legislature.—Joseph R. Brown was a member of the first Territorial Legislature. Most of the others were fur traders who knew nothing about the organization of a great common-wealth. So they made Joseph Brown secretary of the Council, as the Upper House was called. With the knowledge he had gained in the Wisconsin Legislature, he managed everything. Having an infectious laugh and a keen sense of humor, he was always the center of a crowd. They nicknamed him "Jo, the Juggler," because he was so clever at getting things done.

Interpreter for Governor Ramsey. —When Governor Ramsey went to Traverse des Sioux for the big treaty with the Indians, Joe Brown was right there, along with the other celebrities of the day.

He went with Governor Ramsey the following year also, when the Governor carried thousands of dollars to Traverse des Sioux to pay the first of the Indian claims. This time he act-

37

ed as interpreter since he could speak the Sioux language fluently, having married an Indian woman. He could associate with savages or rule a political caucus with equal ease.

Takes over St. Paul paper.—After Goodhue died, Joe Brown took over the St. Paul newspaper and made a big impression as an editor. He was a large man with a Roman nose, prominent chin and thin lips and strong bright eyes. Though his head was slightly bald on top, his hair hung down in long waves.

Being the editor, he got a job printing the legislative bills which made him a lot of extra money. He could dash off pages of editorials without having to change a word. He spoke and read French easily.

Develops new communities. — He could not be content in one place very long. Communities were being developed in various sections of the state. He started a community in southwestern Minnesota called Brown's Valley. Then he moved to a place between Renville and Sacred Heart and built a mansion. The walls were of red granite, and so thick the window sills made good seats. There were wide balconies across the front and sides. There were twenty rooms and in the attic he had a billiard table and his desk. The parlor had black mohair furniture, bronze chandeliers and heavy damask curtains. There was a piano in the parlor and another one in Mrs. Brown's sitting room. There was a gardener, a coachman, and a barn worker. The overseer had a small separate house. They kept two maids and an Indian woman for the housework.

They built this elegant place with Indian scrip which Mrs. Brown received.

They had elaborate parties in the big house when guests danced the Virginia Reel, the Wahpeton Waltz and the Sisseton Schottische, the melodies interwoven with Dakota love songs.

Joins Sibley's army.—They lived in the beautiful house for only a year until the Indian massacres occurred. Then it was destroyed. Joseph Brown raised a company to help defend the frontier. He was sent out of New Ulm with his company to bury the dead and bring in refugees. The Indians caught him unprepared and although Joe Brown thought he knew Indian

…eam Wagon.

ways, there were a large number of casualties.

He moved to Henderson to establish a new town and became the editor of the paper. He also ran a stage from Henderson to St. Paul.

His steam wagon. — Then he became interested in making a wagon that would run faster than the slow-moving Red River carts. He wanted it to deliver freight across the prairies. The wagon ran without being pulled and looked something like one of our present-day traction engines. It depended on wood for fuel and the mechanism was made by a blacksmith. Though it was very cumber-some, it could pull ten to thirty tons.

Mr. Brown planned on making six machines to run to six different trading posts. He planned to construct roads with wood and water stations along the way. In an exhibition run, he drove it through the streets of Henderson and everyone ran out to see what Joseph R. Brown was up to. On the edge of town, they tried to cross a bog and the machine sank so deeply into the mud they could not get it out. Mr. Brown would not give up. He worked on his idea the rest of his life and put all his money into it. He never really got his idea perfected before he died.

CHAPTER ELEVEN

Colonel Josiah Snelling
Commandant

Those who have seen Fort Snelling in its prominent position at the junction of the Mississippi and Minnesota Rivers between Minneapolis and St. Paul will find it hard to realize it started with a few men who had to build cabins before they could have shelter from the weather.

In 1820 Colonel Josiah Snelling, a peppery, red-headed man who had served in the War of 1812 with distinction, came to command the new Fort. You will remember that Pike had bought the site from the Indians for $2000 when he had made his explorations fifteen years before. At that time, the Military Department wanted this place as one in a chain of frontier defense.

Leavenworth started to build. — Colonel Henry Leavenworth had been sent to the Fort the year before Snelling. He had ordered the first buildings erected on the flats along the Minnesota River. He called the place New Hope. But these buildings were not put up to withstand a Minnesota winter. The roof of one cabin blew off entirely. They never had enough to eat. Scurvy broke out and forty died from this awful disease. In the spring the camp was moved across the

40

river and named Camp Coldwater because of a spring by that name. Then Colonel Leavenworth was ordered to another place and Colonel Snelling came as commander.

A new location.—The Snellings had just reached Camp Coldwater when their fifth child was born. Mrs. Snelling's room was papered and carpeted with buffalo skins. Immediately Colonel Snelling decided the Fort should be at the top of the hill. The soldiers were carpenters and stone masons as well as defenders. Removing the white limestone from the side of the big hill, they built a round tower with slits so rifles could be fired in all directions. The white sandstone building stood out against the green woods and the sparkling water below. It allowed a view of the valley for miles. To the south lay the fertile valley of the St. Peter, as the Minnesota River was then called. All about were roll-

Round Tower.

ing prairies, green woods and lovely knolls.

Resident buildings and others had to be made of wood, but the hospital was made of stone. Soldiers had to chop trees for building. They could not prepare lumber fast enough by hand.

First sawmill established.—Colonel Snelling established a sawmill at the Falls of St. Anthony. That was the first use of the enormous water power, although more than a hundred

First Saw Mill.

41

years had passed since its first discovery. The site for the mill was a few rods below the brink of the St. Anthony Falls on the west bank of the river. The structure was about twenty feet square and two stories high. The Colonel sent to St. Louis for a quick-acting, upright saw called a "Muley." This hastened the building and by fall most of the soldiers had quarters and were working on buildings for the officers. Lumber from the Falls was used to make furniture as well as housing. During those first years there were shortages of everything, and they had to think of ways to supply themselves from the things at hand. Once when they got short of writing paper, the quartermaster made his reports to Washington on birch bark.

Each soldier became a farmer.— As soon as everyone had a place to live, Colonel Snelling had the men plant wheat and corn. Each man had to cultivate a garden also. He believed that men must keep busy if they were to be happy.

The wheat came up all right, but they had no place to grind it.

Grinding mill installed. — Colonel Snelling sent to St. Louis for millstones and equipment for a flour mill. His men installed one run of millstones, or burrs, and the necessary shafting. A small home for the miller was built next door to the mill. Water for turning the wheels of the mill was carried through a wooden flume. The first grinding of flour

Minnehaha Falls

was so poor they could not use it. However, it was soon improved upon. The government operated both the flour and sawmill for twenty-eight years.

Life takes on a routine.—Back of the fort the herds of cattle kept to supply meat for the men grazed quietly.

The stars and stripes were run up every morning and lowered at night. Mrs. Snelling started a Sunday School for the children. So many soldiers attended that she started an adult class and they studied the lives of the patriarchs of the Bible. People at the Fort entertained themselves with trips to Minnehaha Falls where deer ran through the fragrant woods.

Flowers and fern grew everywhere. In season, they went to gather wild strawberries where the city of Minneapolis now stands. They drove to Lake Calhoun for fishing. In winter, when icicles hung from the eaves and snow lay deep, they were cut off from the rest of the world. Then they gave plays, song-fests and parties. People came to them from St. Anthony and St. Paul.

The mail was brought up from Prairie du Chien by messenger on horseback. It was supposed to come once a week, but one winter when the snow was very deep, they got no mail for five months. Just the same the soldiers had to leave the Fort on several occasions to help settlers in distress.

Mrs. Snelling

The river monster.—One morning there was a strange new sound. They saw smoke on the river. It was a steamboat named "Virginia." This was the first steamer that had ever reached the Fort. Cannons boomed a welcome. The Indians declared their sacred men had dreamed of seeing a monster on the waters. They were sure this was it. When it puffed hot steam and the big paddle wheels splashed water in every direction, they knew it was a bad spirit. They called it a fire canoe. Indian mothers sought hiding places for their children and chiefs forgot their dignity and ran away.

All the whites ran down to the levee. There was confusion and splashing and clinking as the gangplank grated on the sand. The people at the Fort could hardly wait until the barrels and bales were unloaded.

General Scott makes a visit.—Up to 1821 the Fort was still known by the name of St. Anthony. Then General Scott made a trip of inspection. The ladies wore beautiful dresses they had brought from the East and the officers wore full dress uniforms to entertain him. Colonel Snelling's seven-year-old son distracted attention away from a review of the troops when he climbed on a hollow log and scared up a nest of bees. He yelled so loud the soldiers had to come to his rescue. Nevertheless General Scott was so impressed with the way Colonel Snelling had carved a fort out of the wilderness that he suggested in Washington that the name be changed to Snelling in his honor. Fort Snelling it has been ever since.

Other steamers on the river.—In a short time nine steamers were making runs from St. Louis to Fort Snelling during the summer months. The name of each boat was elaborately painted on the shield over the wheel. Because they could not get through during the winter, it was always a big event when the first one arrived in the spring. How people hurried to the landing to get news and mail from home! How the women welcomed the fresh food after living on codfish and dried apples! How glad they were to get cloth for new dresses!

By 1826 there were 214 soldiers at Fort Snelling. In 1828 Colonel Snelling died in Washington.

Old Fort.

Commander's Quarters

CHAPTER TWELVE

Pond Brothers

Missionaries

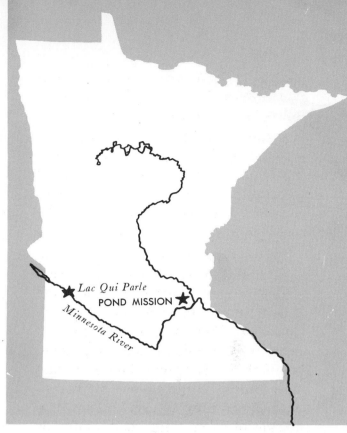

Lac Qui Parle
POND MISSION
Minnesota River

When the Pond Brothers came to Minnesota, the white population of the whole territory consisted of the soldiers at the Fort and a few scattered traders. The Ponds were not ordained ministers but had simply received a call to act as missionaries to the Indians. For that reason, they did not have a license from any religious organization but they had a strong desire to bring Christianity to the

Sioux, or Dakotas, as they were often called.

Gideon Pond teaches plowing. — Major Taliaferro, who was the Indian agent near Fort Snelling, had been trying to teach agriculture to the Indians. He had already given a plow to the tribe at Kaposia, near future St. Paul. The Indians did not have the least idea how to use it. Major Taliaferro suggested that Gideon Pond go there and teach them how to plow.

Carrying his own food, Gideon went to Kaposia. He showed the chief how to harness a pony to the plow and how to hold it so it would turn the furrows. When it came time to eat, he found that his food had disappeared, stolen either by dogs or Indians. As a result, he had to eat with the Indians and could hardly swallow the things they gave him. He had to sleep in one of their wigwams and it was infested with lice. When the sun came up, the dogs set up a terrific barking. He was glad when a few of the tribe had mastered the use of the plow so he could return to the fort.

Build mission school. — The two brothers wanted to build a mission school where they could teach and convert the Indians. Major Taliaferro told them there was a tribe camped near Lake Calhoun and they could build there. However, he asked that they teach farming along with religion. When they agreed, he lent them a team of oxen, a log chain and tools to build with. He also donated a window for their house. They bought some nails which came to a shilling and that was all they spent on their house.

They built it of oak logs, overlooking Lake Calhoun where the loons called and the blackbirds gathered. The cabin was 12 by 16 feet with a dug-out cellar and a low attic. The bark roof was tied to tamarack poles with strips of basswood. It was divided into two rooms with floors of split logs. They covered the logs with wolf skins to keep the floor warm. They enclosed four acres with a split rail fence to keep out the deer and other animals that wanted to eat the things they planted.

The first winter Gideon cut logs and pulled them to the cabin with the oxen. Samuel cut them into the right size for their fireplace.

Hold first services.—Of course, the Indians hung around all the time, anxious to see what the white men were doing. The Pond brothers invited all of them to opening exercises. They read from the Bible and prayed. Someone had to interpret everything they said. Then they had a banquet of tough mussels from the lake. However, this little cabin was the first mission and school for the Dakota Indians.

Friendly Indians. — Indians were always around. One would come to borrow an axe, another, a hatchet. Another would want the use of a trap or to have a stick split. Women and children screamed at the blackbirds that tried to eat everything they planted. Indians often gathered near the mission by the hundreds to play ball. After the braves had been away on a hunting trip, they went at once to Pond's Mission to shake hands, expecting a warm welcome back.

They learn the Sioux language.— The big problem of the Pond brothers was to learn the Sioux language. It was hard to make the Indians understand their messages through interpreters. Gideon was so anxious to learn that he went with some of the band on a duck hunt. Every time he learned a new word he wrote it down in a little notebook he carried. Unfortunately the Dakotas and the Chippewas from the north fought every time they met. This time Gideon's companions ran into some Chippewas. Several Indians were killed and Gideon was lucky to escape with his life.

He kept on with his task of making a Dakota dictionary. His ears were alert to every new word he could get. The Indians called him "Grizzly Bear." They called Samuel "Red Eagle."

It wasn't easy to convert the Indians. They were devout in their own way, but they were entirely under the influence of the Medicine Man and everything he told them they thought was infallible. So the missionaries had to destroy all their old suspicions while they sowed the seed of Christianity. They had to translate the Scriptures into Dakota before they could present their teachings. They had to fight the greed of the traders. They also found many of the Indian agents were indifferent to the needs of the Redmen.

New mission established.—Neither of the Pond Brothers was much in-

og Cabin.

terested in teaching the Indians to farm. They had come to save souls. So they spent more and more time on their Indian dictionary and teaching the Bible.

They had lived in their cabin almost a year and could converse quite easily with the savages when Rev. Thomas Williamson, who was also a doctor, came to the Fort. With him was Rev. Stevens and a Mr. Huggins who was prepared to teach agriculture. Dr. Williamson and Rev. Stevens were assigned to a site on the shore of Lake Harriet, only about a mile from the Ponds. The Pond brothers went to help them build a cabin.

Shortly after Dr. Williamson was sent to Lac qui Parle, leaving Rev. Stevens in charge. Rev. Stevens suggested that the Pond brothers move in with him to form a combined mission since they were so close together. The brothers hated to leave the place they had built up with their toil but they finally consented. They moved to the Harriet mission, taking along their cow and corn and potatoes they had raised in their garden.

The brothers separate. — They did not get along very well with Rev. Stevens so after one winter, Gideon went to Lac qui Parle to join Rev. Williamson. Samuel returned East to study theology so he could be ordained. After a year of study he returned to Harriet Mission as a regular minister and was married to Miss Cordelia Eggleston, the sister of Mrs.

Pond Farm.

Stevens. The wedding was held in the Mission House. Many came from the Fort, including the surgeon, Dr. Emerson, who was Dred Scott's master. The bridesmaid was Mr. Steven's sister. The best man was Henry Sibley. It was the bride's twenty-third birthday. Rev. Stevens performed the ceremony.

By this time Samuel was getting $200.00 a year salary from the missionary society. The couple set up housekeeping in a small room over the mission school. Their first teapot was an old oil can.

United at Harriet Mission. — The next year Gideon came to see Samuel. He came from Lac qui Parle by canoe and brought along his wife and baby. The Stevens family was transferred to another mission and the Pond brothers ran the Lake Harriet Mission alone. By then, Samuel Pond had 3000 words in a dictionary and had completed a small Indian grammar.

He carried a small bottle of ink with him wherever he went. He made quill pens to write with so he could add to his dictionary on any occasion.

Samuel and his wife adopted a little Indian girl who grew up to marry a white man.

Gideon Pond held an afternoon Sunday service for whites at his mission. People often drove the ten miles from the Fort to hear him.

Samuel at Shakopee.—The Harriet Mission was disbanded and Gideon went back to Lac qui Parle for a time. Samuel went to Shakopee. It was a hard place for his wife. The Indians walked into the house whenever they felt like it, tracking in mud and making their picture writings on the wall. His wife took sick and died there. Samuel had to forget his own grief to be both doctor and minister to the Indians. He cured them of croup and other ailments and vaccinated them against smallpox.

Gideon at Oak Grove. — Gideon Pond was moved to Bloomington, a few miles west of Fort Snelling. It was called the Oak Grove Mission. Though the two brothers were only about fourteen miles apart, they seldom got to see each other since they were both so busy. Gideon lost his wife shortly after Samuel's died. Later Gideon married Mrs. Hopkins whose missionary husband drowned during the Traverse des Sioux treaty meeting.

The Ponds left their mark because they wrote the language of the Indians. Their notes recorded the life of the period. They taught the Indians to live civilized lives and increased understanding between the tribes and the whites.

48

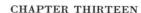

CHAPTER THIRTEEN

Major Stephen H. Lon

Topographical Engineer

Because the Secretary of War decided in 1817 that the frontier line should be examined, the task of surveying the upper Mississippi River was delegated to Major Stephen H. Long of the topographical engineers. This was strictly a scientific exploration. In the group was a zoologist, a geologist, and a landscape painter. They came up the river from St. Louis in a six-oared skiff. When they reached Minnesota, they hired Joseph Renville as a guide.

Long's assignment.—Major Long's assignment was to pick suitable places for forts which could protect the trade and preserve frontier peace. He stopped at the camp of Chief Wabasha and made friends. Then he went to Kaposia near the present site of St.

Paul and found a big tribe. They wore long hair with vermillion parts and skirts of calico. They had both winter and summer homes. The summer houses were made of saplings covered with bark. Outside was a platform sheltered by a roof of boughs. There were shelves along the platform where they could sit during the day and sleep at night. In the spring they went to sugar camps. The men hunted muskrats while the women made

49

Indian Village.

sugar. They returned to camp in time to plant corn.

When cold froze the swamps and made the rivers lifeless, they went into winter houses. These were teepees of leather with straw piled outside to shut out the wind. Straw was scattered over the ground inside and covered with fur rugs.

While Long was there they did the Bear Dance for him. This was to initiate a boy into manhood. They painted the story of his dream on a flag made from the skin of a fawn. They suspended this from a flagpole with a pipe dangling underneath. At the foot of the pole were two arrows and fragments of painted feathers. Nearby was the bear hole about two feet deep. The young hero got into the hole.

Other young men, dressed in their best, pretended to hunt for him. As they approached the boy leaped from the hole with two hoops and wooden lances. He danced around the pole,

exhibiting various feats while the other boys tried to trap him. He could use any form of violence to get away from them. In the end he fled to the woods for the rest of the day.

If they had caught him, he would have had to stay in a lodge for the rest of the day and they would have performed sacred rites over him. Either way it went, he was considered a man from then on.

The future site of Fort Snelling.— Long picked the future site of Fort Snelling. He went from there to explore the Minnesota River which was then called St. Peter's. They went by water to Traverse des Sioux. They had four canoes. Some of the men walked along the river bank instead of canoeing. After exploring the Minnesota River, they followed the Red River clear up to Pembina on the Canadian border. The astronomer ascertained their position and marked the boundary between United States and Canada.

Chief Wabasha.

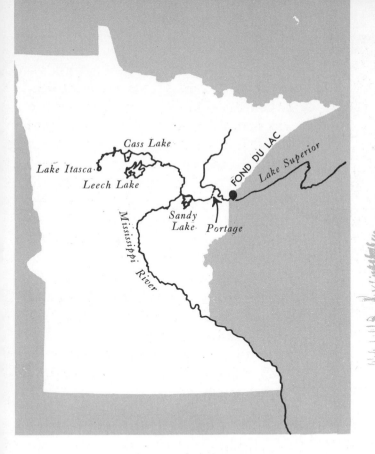

CHAPTER FOURTEEN

Henry Schoolcraft
Geologist . . . Mineralogist

In 1832 Henry Schoolcraft, Indian agent from the Sault Ste. Marie, with a party of thirty men, came west into Minnesota. This was then a part of Michigan territory. They wanted to visit the Indians, vaccinate them, and try to promote friendship between the Sioux and the Chippewas.

The journey.—In the party were some soldiers, a physician, an interpreter and a missionary named Rev. William T. Boutwell. They carried provisions and gifts for the Indians. They went to Fond du Lac and up the St. Louis River. They portaged around some falls where the dense forests were full of bogs. Sometimes they waded in water up to their knees. When they made a portage, they had to carry everything on their backs,

even the canoes. They saw Chippewa signals along the way. These were drawings on stakes driven into the ground. Finally they reached Sandy Lake. Then they went up the Mississippi River to Leech Lake.

At Leech Lake.—For thirteen years Schoolcraft had been wanting to get to Leech Lake. Thirteen years before he had covered some of the same ter-

Camping by lake.

Exploring by canoe.

ritory with Cass who was then Governor of Michigan. At that time Schoolcraft had kept records of the trip and received $1.50 a day for his work. Governor Cass had been sure that Cass Lake, named after him, was the source of the Mississippi River. All those thirteen years Schoolcraft had refused to believe Cass Lake was the source of the great river. He had read about the explorations of Major Long and others and no one had told of finding another source. So Schoolcraft was overjoyed to make this trip into Minnesota to find out for himself where the Mississippi really did rise.

Reverend Boutwell's headquarters.

Canoeing through rapids.

He searches farther. — When Schoolcraft reached Cass Lake, he talked to some of the Indians through his interpreters. They told him Cass Lake was not the source of the Mississippi River. They showed him an inlet flowing in from the west. Schoolcraft and his men followed this inlet and came out at another lake.

The new lake.—They explored this new lake and finding no inlet, decided this must be the real source. Rev. Boutwell shortened and combined two Latin words meaning "truth" and "head" and formed the word **Itasca.**

Today, if you visit in the area of Lake Itasca or Cass Lake, you will find a great deal of forest country which is much like it was in those days.

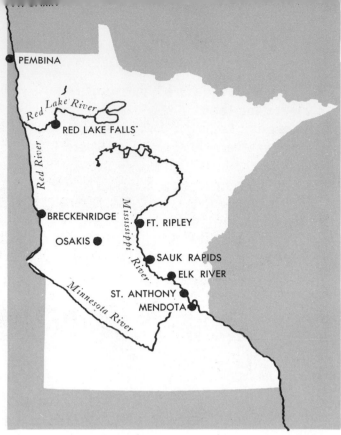

CHAPTER FIFTEEN

Pierre Bottineau

Guide . . . Voyageur
Interpreter

Pierre Bottineau, a big bear of a man with shaggy black hair, fierce eyebrows and a heavy beard, knew most of Minnesota territory from first hand experience. He served many years as a guide.

First experiences. — He was little more than a boy when he got his first experience on the trail. At that time he helped carry messages from Fort Garry in Canada to Fort Snelling. He followed the Red River to a point across the Territory from Fort Snelling and then went across country.

At this particular time he accompanied an older man named Le Compte. As usual, they followed the east bank of the Red River to a point near East Grand Forks of today. Here they had to cross Red Lake River.

Although ice was forming on the water, they built a big raft and young Bottineau took the mail, baggage and provisions across. He returned to get Le Compte who was on horseback because of lameness. Astride the pony's back on the raft with Pierre holding the bridle, they were almost across when they got caught in the current. Le Compte was thrown from the horse and all of them were pitched into the river. The horse managed to swim to shore and Bottineau saved

Le Compte but it was a harrowing experience for them.

Going on, they got lost on several occasions, their food gave out, and they were almost starving by the time they reached Fort Snelling.

Returning to Fort Garry, Bottineau trapped, hunted buffalo and led a wild life. Then he married a girl from the Red River settlement. To make some money, he herded twenty head of cattle down to Mr. Sibley at Mendota. He received about fifty dollars apiece for the cows. While there, he helped Father Galtier build his little chapel at St. Paul.

Learning that an imaginary line had been set up to keep the Sioux and Chippewas apart, he built a cabin on the dividing line. He called it "Sakis,"

which meant danger spot. The town of Osakis grew there.

In 1841 he bought claims in the very heart of future St. Paul, and immediately a French settlement sprang up around his location.

Starts a freighting system. — The next year he went to St. Anthony and began to operate some mackinaw boats, rigged for both rowing and sailing. The boats were manned by eight voyageurs and each carried four tons. The goods were done up in eighty-pound parcels and when the voyageurs had to make a portage, each man carried two bundles. These boats ran between St. Anthony and Sauk Rapids. He added some larger, flat-bottomed boats to transfer goods from St. Anthony to Fort Ripley for the

Hunting for buffalo.

One buffalo on prairie.

American Fur Company and the United States Government.

In 1847 General Isaac Stevens sought a right of way for a Pacific railway and Pierre Bottineau was his guide. Whenever he met Indians, his hand was raised in the sign of peace.

Settles in St. Anthony. — Wishing to have his family with him, he bought frontage on the east side of the Mississippi River near St. Anthony Falls for $150. He brought his family to St. Anthony and they lived in a tepee the first summer. By winter he had built a cabin and the next summer he had planted twenty acres in grain. Another French settlement grew up around him. He donated two full blocks of his property to St. Anthony of Padua Church.

Invests in real estate. — Bottineau built a trading post on the bluff at Elk River and opened a hotel in connection with the post. He continued to buy land around St. Anthony. Soon the entire east side waterfront belonged either to him or Franklin Steele. Together they hired a surveyor to lay out a town. The surveyor's name was Mr. Marshall. Neither Bottineau or Steele dreamed that Mr. Marshall would some day be Governor of Minnesota.

He moves to Bottineau Prairie. — In 1852 he moved his family to a farm which he called Bottineau Prairie. Since he had twenty-eight children, they needed a farm to live on. Soon he was again surrounded by friends and neighbors and the town of Osseo was born.

In 1853 he got up a big buffalo hunt for some visiting English lords and bankers who wanted a taste of this wild sport.

In 1856 he took a group to locate the town of Breckenridge.

In 1861 he guided Governor Ramsey when he went to Pembina to sign an Indian treaty.

In 1863 he led a party in a preliminary survey of a proposed route to the west coast for the Northern Pacific Railroad. He not only served as guide but hunted for them as well.

In retirement. — In his last years he retired to a farm near Red Lake Falls in Polk County. There he led a patriarchal life, surrounded by his many children and grandchildren. He could speak five languages, had talked with the famous men of his time, yet he never took the trouble to learn to read and write.

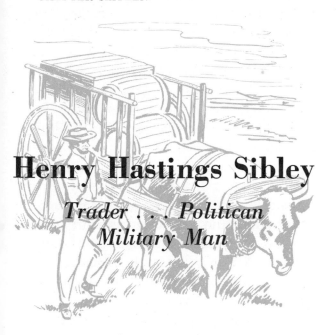

CHAPTER SIXTEEN

Henry Hastings Sibley

Trader . . . Politican Military Man

If you ever visit the Sibley House at Mendota, you will see a beautiful building restored by the Minnesota Daughters of the American Revolution. It is filled with relics of Sibley occupancy, portraits of early settlers and objects of historic interest. In fact, it is often called the Mount Vernon of Minnesota.

Sibley at Mendota.—Henry Hastings Sibley came to Mendota in November of 1834 just six months after the Pond Brothers. He was then in his twenty-third year. He was sent as a partner of the American Fur Company and had been attracted to the job because it promised good hunting and fishing. It was one of his duties to buy furs from the trappers and Indians, check them at Mendota, and then ship them to St. Louis and points east, to be sent all over the world. In exchange Sibley furnished remote traders with merchandise to be used in Indian trade. Most of the white people lived around Fort Snelling or St. Anthony Falls. They traveled back and forth across the river by means of a ferry boat.

Sibley's mansion. — Sibley hired men to build a big house for him on the river. It was built of blue limestone with walls two feet thick and big porches on the front. The plaster was made of mud and clay from the river bank, held together with twisted grass and wooden pegs. On the outside there were steps leading up to the third story where Indians could spend the night if they wished. Sometimes as many as thirty Indians slept up there at once.

Sibley lived like a lord. — Sibley lived like a lord, dressed in velvet and broadcloth. He stamped the wax on his letters with a gold seal. Sibley

Sibley House

Interior of House.

House was like a royal court on the frontier and he was a border baron. Yet his big front room was piled to the ceiling with blankets, bolts of calico, beads and tobacco. Often any extra spaces were crammed with strong-smelling furs and dogs were in every room for he loved hunting dogs as well as horses. He kept a Negro cook and entertained military men, explorers and traders.

A wealth of furs.—It is said he collected $58,000 in furs the first year. He accumulated the riches of the forest with the help of traders, clerks, voyageurs and Indians. At the same time, he was generous with favors and hospitality, the "Tall Trader" to all who knew him. The Indians held him in great respect. He was a handsome six-footer with black hair and brown eyes. He spoke Sioux as easily as French and English. He had a hunting shack near the present city of Austin. During one winter his party shot 2000 deer, 50 elk, 50 bear and several

buffalo. Sibley often went on hunting trips with the Indians.

Sibley's friends.—You may recall how Renville had established a trading post at Lac qui Parle where he also reigned as a king. Sometimes Sibley went to see Renville. Once he gave him five volumes of the History of England and the Biography of Napoleon. Renville came to Sibley's post every spring to exchange his furs for trade goods to last a year.

About that time Franklin Steele was lumbering along the St. Croix River. Sibley was made a Justice of the Peace. His territory was as large as France. Boundaries changed often during those days and he received mail addressed to the Territory of Michigan, Wisconsin, Iowa and Minnesota at various times.

Sibley marries.—In 1843 Mr. Sibley married the sister of Franklin Steele. His wife immediately set about to change things. The big front room was no longer used for storage or an office. She had it cleaned and papered

Mrs. Sibley

and ordered heavy mahogany furniture. She refurnished the entire house. She hired more help in the kitchen so she could entertain all the celebrities that came to their home. They put on elaborate feasts, serving guests with buffalo hump, dried beaver tails that tasted like dried beef, wild game and vegetables from their own garden.

Men who worked for Sibley. — Great creaking Red River carts continued to bring furs to Mendota. The drivers were mostly half-breeds who wore coonskin caps, buckskin trousers and jumpers. They added bright sashes and headbands. Clerks received $200 a year. Interpreters were paid $150 a year. Voyageurs got $100.

Sibley goes to Washington. — In 1848 Sibley went to Washington to get Minnesota admitted into the Union as a Territory. People in Washington were surprised when he appeared in fine clothes. They had expected him to come in buckskins. He reported to Congress that the territory known as Minnesota had forests, prairies and waterways. He claimed it could become a leader in agriculture since the soil was adapted to raising grain. He told them it had water and minerals. He reported that lumbering had begun and the climate, though variable, was healthful and pleasant. He urged that Minnesota be admitted to the Union.

The new Governor.—In 1849 Minnesota Territory was admitted. The new governor, Alexander Ramsey, was appointed to set up the government of the Territory. There was no place in St. Paul for him and his wife to stay so the Sibleys entertained them for a month.

Sibley becomes a Governor.—Nine years later, when Minnesota became a state, Sibley was the first state governor. The Sibleys left their Mendota home and moved to St. Paul. It was a difficult time for Sibley because the state was going through the depression. There was not a mile of railroads. There were no sound banks and no money in the state treasury. The harvest was almost a failure. Everyone was gloomy and fearful. Newspapers were filled with notices of mortgage foreclosures.

Sibley fights the Sioux.—Governor Ramsey was elected to serve again and when the Sioux Uprising occurred, he called on Sibley to take charge of the Minnesota regiments and go against the Indians. Sibley had hunted and fished with the red men and knew them intimately. He hated to go against them in battle. But he accepted the position and organized an army to conquer the marauders. He subdued the Indians, restored 250 whites who had been captured and took 2000 Indians, driving the others outside the state. Minnesota has a number of places named for this great man. There is a Sibley County, Sibley Street in St. Paul, the town of Sibley and Sibley State Park.

CHAPTER SEVENTEEN

Reverend Doctor Williamson
Missionary

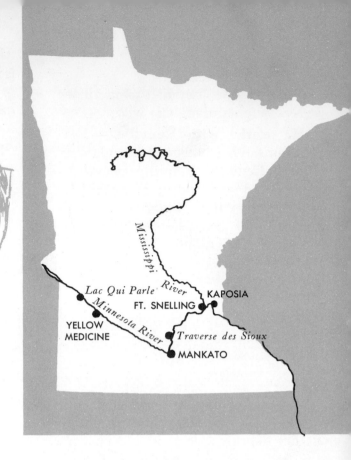

The Pond Brothers had been at Lake Calhoun about a year when Rev. Williamson, who was both a minister and a doctor, came to Fort Snelling in the summer of 1835. He had been sent by the American Board of Commissioners for Foreign Missions. With him was the Rev. J. D. Stevens, a farmer named Alexander Huggins, and two teachers.

Rev. Williamson lived at Fort Snelling for several months. While there, he organized the First Presbyterian Church and Mr. Sibley, who had been a church member in Michi-

gan, became one of the deacons.

At Lac qui Parle.—Rev. Williamson was sent to Lac qui Parle where Joseph Renville had his fort. Here he established a mission. It was a hard trip from Fort Snelling clear across the State to Lac qui Parle. The Williamsons loaded all their goods on a wagon and put the wagon on a flatboat which floated them down to Traverse des Sioux. There they took the wagon off the boat and started across the prairie to Lac qui Parle. Once a rawhide strap broke and the cart tipped. It dumped out the family and baggage. At another time they were trying to get through a slough. An ox went down, bellowing in fear. The family ran from turf to turf till they got to dry ground. They finally got the ox out. They had to camp out several nights along the way.

He works with Renville. — Rev. Williamson became good friends with Joseph Renville. Renville joined his church and was a ruling member. The next summer Rev. Riggs came to join the Lac qui Parle mission. Then Gideon Pond came to help.

They organized the Hazelwood Republic and any Indian who wanted to belong had to cut off his long hair, wear clothing like the whites and attend church. Indians who met the requirements of Hazelwood Mission were known as civilized Indians. Others were called blanket Indians.

The three missionaries worked together to build up a good mission center with a school, church and other buildings. Provisions were a heavy expense. They tried to raise enough grain and vegetables to carry them through the year. In 1837 they bought a small grinding mill so they could grind their wheat and corn.

Translating the Bible. — Their biggest task was the translating of the Bible into the language of the Indians. Joseph Renville gave them much assistance. Rev. Williamson would read a verse, Renville would translate it into Dakota, and Pond would write it down. Following that method they also made hymn books and catechisms.

Doctor Williamson's preaching was different from other ministers. He used simple words and short sentences. His talks were very effective.

In front of Rev. Williamson's home at Yellow Medicine

At Little Crow's village. — In 1846 Renville died and Little Crow, whose tribe lived at Kaposia near St. Paul, asked that Mr. Williamson be moved there to start a mission. Rev. Williamson left Lac qui Parle in charge of Rev. Riggs and went to Kaposia. There he built a church with a steeple and a bell. He was much more than a minister because he used his medical knowledge to help those who needed it. In time he also added a boarding school for Indian children.

After the Indian outbreak when Little Crow and his men were ringleaders, the Kaposia band was broken up and the Indians were all moved to Yellow Medicine County. It meant a lot of grief for the innocent ones to have to leave their homes and the graves of their dear ones. The guilty Indians were held at Mankato to await punishment. Doctor Williamson moved to Yellow Medicine with the tribe but every week he went to Mankato to preach to the jailed men. He died in St. Peter in 1877 when he was eighty years old.

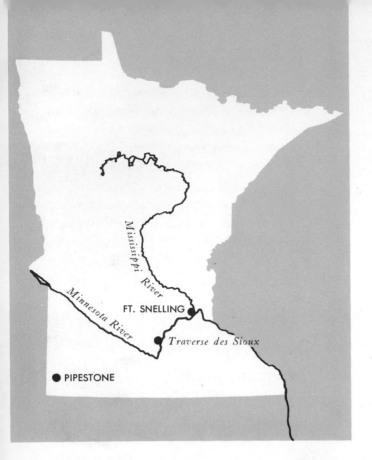

CHAPTER EIGHTEEN

George Catlin

Artist . . . Explorer

George Catlin, who painted Indian people and scenes, came to Fort Snelling in 1835. He requested Major Taliaferro to arrange some sort of Indian gathering so he could get pictures of them.

Major Taliaferro told the Indians that his guest was a powerful Medicine Man and promised to have the cannon at the Fort fired twenty-one times if they would put on a Fourth of July celebration for Catlin.

Hundreds of Indians gathered, all dressed in bright clothing decorated with beads and feathers. Catlin presented each one with a small gift. Then rival teams of Sioux and Chippewas played La Crosse with long sticks. After the game, they did the Buffalo Dance, the Beggar, Bear and

Eagle Dances. In the Eagle Dance, the braves dressed in eagle feathers.

In the evening, Taliaferro had the cannon fired as he had promised. Each Indian got a gift of tobacco, pork or flour before leaving. During their performances Catlin had been drawing them in every sort of activity and had a good variety of pictures to finish up.

He paints Indians and scenery. — They allowed him to use a room at the Fort as a studio. He worked there for hours every day. When the weather permitted, he went up and down the river by canoe, painting scenery. Later he put all his work into a book.

The Indian pipes. — Catlin was intrigued by the Indian pipes because they were carved with elaborate al-

The Red Man Is Part of the Red Stone"

Great Spirit, Gitchi-Manitou, who has his throne at Pipestone. He gave that place to the Indians so that they might go there for peace pipes."

Another Indian told Catlin of the legend of the quarries. He said, "One day a number of Dakotas gathered to dig the stone. It was a sultry evening with clouded skies. The Indians, sensing a storm, sought shelter. The storm came and when they looked toward the quarry, they saw a pillar of smoke and the outline of a giant moving back and forth with one arm pointed heavenward. Lightning flashed and the figure disappeared. On going to the place next morning, they found figures and images drawn on the walls. Since then it has been a sacred place."

Winnewissa Falls at Pipestone

legorical designs on bowls and stems. He was told that the stone came from a quarry clear across the territory. He decided he would find the quarry.

He started down the Minnesota River but when he got to Traverse des Sioux, some Indians tried to keep him from going on.

Warned away from quarries. — They warned him not to trespass on the sacred fountain of the pipe. "No white man has ever gazed on the quarries and no white man ever will," they told him. They explained that even the Indians who went to get the stone had to go through purification rituals first.

One Indian held out his arm. "See," he said. "The red man is part of the red stone. It was given to them by the

In spite of warnings. — Catlin listened respectfully to their warnings but went to Pipestone anyway. He left the Minnesota River on horseback, going southeast with a companion. He came upon the mine suddenly. It was a thirty-foot wall that ran for two miles. It looked like a great red jewel on folds of green velvet. Figures of snakes, rabbits and other creatures were carved on some of the rocks.

From the heart of the ridge a waterfall gushed. The water was so clear the rocks showed through.

Named Catlinite.—Catlin chopped off a few pieces of the rock and sent them to a Boston chemist who decided it was something new and called it Catlinite for Catlin. The name was later changed to Pipestone. Today you may visit Pipestone National Monument and see the place where the Indians dug the stone for their beautiful pipes.

Along Minnesota River.

This stone carried the tribute of peaceful relations around a thousand campfires. Whenever Indians went and conferred with white men, the discussions were always solemnized by smoking the peace pipe or calumet.

Peace Cairn at Pipestone quarry.

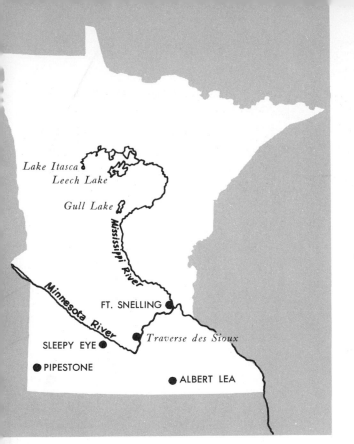

CHAPTER NINETEEN

Joseph Nicolas Nicolle

Geologist
Cartographer

You will find the name of Nicollet attached to a county, several lakes, a large island above the Falls of St. Anthony, a street in Minneapolis and a town in Minnesota. They are all in honor of Joseph Nicolas Nicollet.

Nicollet comes to survey.—Having already received a decoration from the Legion of Honor as an astronomer, Joseph Nicollet came to Minnesota in 1836 to do surveying and explore the sources of the Mississippi. He went first to Fort Snelling and traveled north from there by way of Gull Lake and Gull River to Leech Lake. Renville's son went along as interpreter.

When they stopped at Leech Lake the children fled screaming at the sight of strange white men, but Rev. Boutwell who ran the mission there,

made the whole party welcome. He was glad to see people from the outside world as it was a lonely post. When the children saw he liked the visitors, they hung around constantly, even coming to peep under their tents to see what was going on inside.

Nicollet makes a map.—Rev. Boutwell told them of a Chippewa guide who would take them to Lake Itasca where Schoolcraft had been four

Deer in Woods.

years earlier. When he got to Lake Itasca, Nicollet made a map which was so accurate, it was used by travelers for years afterwards. With tents pitched on Schoolcraft Island, he explored the whole basin of Lake Itasca. Tamarack grew tall and in season the Chippewas gathered there to pick blueberries. He made such good maps of every place he went that they were his monument to posterity. This was not an easy task since he had to plod through dense growths over very rough country. They often saw deer and other wild animals.

Nicollet carried his sextant on his back and his barometer on his left shoulder. Under his arm he had his portfolio and in his hand a basket containing his thermometer, chronometer, pocket compass, artificial horizon and tapeline. On his right shoulder was his spyglass, powder flask and shot bag. In his right hand, he had his gun and umbrella.

The Indians were disappointed when they found he carried no presents for them. They were disgusted at the way he spent most of his time

looking through a tube at the sky. His health was poor and he sacrificed a lot to get his information first hand. At Schoolcraft Island he fixed the latitude and longitude and the height above sea level.

He visits Boutwell.—Returning to Lake Itasca where Rev. Boutwell lived among the somber depths of the pines, he stopped for another visit with that good missionary. Rev. Boutwell took him to see a wild rice harvest.

The Indians had already tied the rice in sheaves so the grains would not fall into the water. They pushed out in boats and with cedar flails, they knocked the grain into their crafts. There were almost a thousand families on the lake and each family got about 25 bushels, leaving plenty for

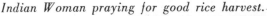
Indian Woman praying for good rice harvest.

ice Harvest.

the ducks and geese. What fell to the bottom of the lake reseeded itself so the rice came up every year without cultivation and made a nutritious food for the Indians.

Tries to teach self-reliance.—Rev. Boutwell explained how he was trying to teach the Indians to provide for themselves instead of looking only one day ahead. He worked all day in his garden while they did nothing. When winter came they tried to beg from him. At first he gave them what they asked for, but at last he adopted the policy of giving each beggar an ax and showing him the woodpile. He told them if they chose to eat and sleep away their summers, they would get nothing free in the winter.

Nicollet returned to Fort Snelling and all that winter he studied the stars from the Round Tower. He stayed with Major Taliaferro and his wife. He was an accomplished violinist and Mrs. Taliaferro accompanied him on the piano. He went almost every day to see Mr. Sibley who took him hunting. He studied the Sioux and Chippewa languages, made field notes and arranged his material.

In the spring he took his scholarly accounts of the geology and resources of Minnesota to Washington. The government appreciated the accuracy of his work. They gave him a commission to return and do more exploring and surveying in Minnesota. This time John C. Fremont was his assistant.

Explores southern Minnesota. — This time his object was to explore southwestern Minnesota. He went through Traverse des Sioux which he said was the site for a future town.

In a lake.

Chief Sleepy Eye.

There he met Joseph Renville and another guide. They had eight Red River carts to carry the luggage and the men. It made quite a caravan. They went south first and founded a small settlement which they named Albert Lea for one of the men in the party. They went northward again to follow the general course of the Minnesota River. Though the weather was hot, the helpers ran races, had wrestling matches, and enjoyed themselves along the way as the oxen plodded over the prairies.

Curious plants.—Watching for curious plants, Nicollet found small yellow flowers which the Indians boiled for dye. There were many compass flowers that grew four feet tall with leaves that always pointed north or south. Some of the men called them rosin plants.

Chief Sleepy Eye.—They met Chief Sleepy Eye who was on a hunting trip. He welcomed the strangers and invited them to visit his home. They agreed to go. Chief Sleepy Eye rode at the head of the caravan, carrying a flag. When they reached his village, his mother came out with a roasted swan, all ready to eat. They parted good friends. They finished their trip at the Catlin stone quarries which are now called Pipestone.

Nicollet explored around Itasca.

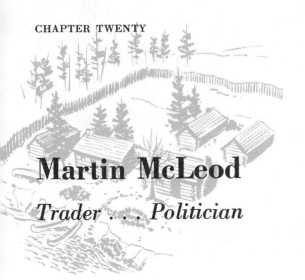

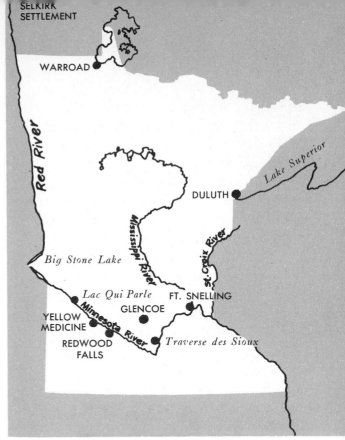

CHAPTER TWENTY

Martin McLeod

Trader . . . Politician

McLeod County in Minnesota is named in memory of one of our famous first men. This was Martin McLeod. When Martin was a young man, he never imagined that he would some day be known as Honorable Martin McLeod. His main interest then was to explore the interesting wilderness countries.

Goes to Selkirk settlement.—There was plenty of talk in Montreal where McLeod lived about the Lord Selkirk settlement on the Red River where

the city of Winnipeg now stands. With a party of twenty-one explorers, he went along to see the Selkirk settlement.

It was a long, hard journey. They went down to Sault Ste. Marie and then followed the shore of Lake Superior in boats. The lake had high wild waves and many times their bateaux were almost upset. One night they stopped to camp on an island and heard singing. They found Indians praying for a safe passage across the lake. They were singing to the Great Spirit, entreating him for fair weather while they crossed.

It took the party nearly three months to reach a point near Duluth, because in spite of the prayers of the Indians it was not all fair weather.

69

Leaving the place now called Duluth they cut across northern Minnesota through heavily wooded lake country. Probably they went to a point near Warroad and then northwest to the Red River Settlement. The distance they covered on foot was over six hundred miles and during that time they each had a pint of rice a day. Once the rice gave out and they had two ounces apiece of meat and a small partridge divided between nine persons.

McLeod starts for Fort Snelling.— The party split up when they got to the Selkirk Settlement and Norman McLeod, with two other young men, decided to go down to Fort Snelling to see if they could get work. Pierre Bottineau, who was going south, agreed to guide them to Lac qui Parle. He told them they could follow the Minnesota River after that.

A terrible trip. — Unfortunately they started in winter. While Bottineau was accustomed to making his way over snowy trails, the boys were not used to winter travel. They carried along some pemmican, expecting to get game along the way. They had to use snowshoes and the straps cut their feet till they bled. They could

seldom make more than ten or fifteen miles a day. Most nights they had to camp out on the prairie. They suffered from the extreme cold. They also suffered for drinking water. Eating snow made them thirstier than ever and caused their mouths to burn with pain.

One of the boys got lost in a sudden blizzard. They never saw him again. The other froze his feet and could not go on. They left him in a cabin while they went to get help but he died there before help came. By the time Norman and Pierre Bottineau reached the Mission at Lac qui Parle, Norman was a saddened young man. Both his friends were dead and he was in a strange country without friends.

At Reverend Williamson's mission. —Doctor Williamson persuaded him to stay at the mission for a few days. Almost overnight there was running water and small flowers stirred the earth. Norman got a chance to go to Fort Snelling in a canoe with some Indians who were taking some dead bodies down that way for burial. Though it wasn't a pleasant trip, he was more than glad to reach Fort Snelling after his harrowing experiences.

He related his experiences to Mr. Sibley and Sibley gave him a job as a clerk. Later Norman went into partnership with another man and started a small trading post near the Fort. His partner died and the winter of 1839, he went up the St. Croix River to trade with the Chippewas.

McLeod's house in Bloomington.

Trading post at Traverse des Sioux.
—He had liked Traverse des Sioux when he had come down from the Selkirk settlement and he decided to return there and open a post. After he got started he went up and down the valley urging the Indians to let him have their furs, scheming to outdo his biggest rival, Joseph R. Brown, who was also trading in that area. Then he did something which was uncommon at that time. Today we are accustomed to chain stores, but Martin McLeod opened a chain of trading posts. While running his various posts with men under him, he was studying history and philosophy. He got his books through Sibley at Mendota.

Becomes an influential man.—He was elected to serve in the first legislature after the Territory of Minnesota was established and received the title of Honorable.

After the treaty of Traverse des Sioux when the Indians were removed to agencies, fur trading was no longer so profitable so he sold all his posts and went into the real estate business.

Proposes a school bill.—While he was a legislator, his dignity and charm made him very influential. It was he who proposed the bill for a school fund so that all youth of Minnesota between the ages of four and twenty-one could get a free education.

He was elected vice-president of the first Historical Society.

Helps locate Glencoe.—In 1855 a number of families came to St. Anthony from the East. They wished to locate in the western part of the state. Mr. McLeod, who knew the country so well, agreed to guide them in search of home sites. With them was Colonel John Stevens.

They went first to where the village of Carver now stands. From there they turned westward but had to chop trees along the way so the teams could get through. They camped at a lake where wild animals prowled about all night. Finding a buffalo trail, they followed it through the forest to the prairie. Soon they had to enter more woods. Fire had swept over that area and every time they touched a plant or tree, soot fell on them.

Again they came out upon prairie. They selected the place that is now Glencoe to carve out a town. Each member selected a claim.

They returned home by way of Traverse des Sioux and the Minnesota River but maintained the Glencoe location was the best of all. The settlers took their families and moved there. In another year there were farms all along the way which they had explored. Thus the city of Glencoe was established under the guidance of Martin McLeod. He worked later to get the town on a growing basis. His letters to friends in Canada brought down many people from there who wished to settle in Minnesota.

CHAPTER TWENTY-ONE

Franklin Steele

Realtor . . . Lumberman
Capitalist

Franklin Steele reached Fort Snelling by canoe in 1837. He came to work as a sutler, or storekeeper. The sutler's job was supposed to furnish an excellent opportunity for a young man in a new country. It placed him on an equal footing with the officers.

Makes investments. — Apparently, Franklin Steele's duties as sutler did not keep him confined to the Fort since he made frequent trips to take up claims and secure lumbering sites. A treaty was pending that year by which the government would get from the Indians the land east of the Mississippi River in Minnesota. Even before the treaty was signed, Franklin Steele was on the St. Croix River, laying claim to valuable water rights by erecting a crude cabin. With a stone fireplace in the center, the smoke went out through a hole in the roof.

Cutting timber. — He had six half-breeds with him and between them they had a cart and one ox. The men cut some timber for Mr. Steele. When a tree was cut down, they loaded it on a bob-sled and the ox dragged it to the top of a slide. When spring came it could be pushed into the water and floated downstream.

They put a chain across the river from shore to shore. This caught the logs so they piled up solid and couldn't get away. They called this a boom. They could walk across a boom as they would on a bridge. But they had to be very careful because sometimes a log would roll and make them fall into the water.

A company is formed. — Steele wanted to go into lumbering in a big way so he went to St. Louis and found men who were interested in forming the St. Croix Lumber Company. The company furnished a saw mill which they sent up the river in a big boat. When the Indians saw the steamboat they threw stones at it. The captain blew a frightful blast on the whistle and the Indians ran away screaming.

The company built a mill and a dam costing $20,000. It was at the rapids where Taylor's Falls now stands. This opened up the towns of Marine and St. Croix Falls. In all those towns sawdust was soon spitting from logs as great blades snarled through.

In 1842 Mr. Steele went to Philadelphia to buy supplies for the sutler's store at the Fort. While in Philadelphia he married and brought his bride back with him. Her sister came along and later married Mr. Sibley.

Mr. Steele's fortunes grow with Minneapolis.—After returning to St. Anthony, he established a ferry across the river. Then he started a sawmill at St. Anthony Falls. By 1848 they were sawing day and night. The wood was taken as soon as it came from the saws because new people were moving in so fast they could not put up homes to supply them all.

The historic year.—The year 1849 was historic for Minneapolis. St. Anthony Falls began to develop as a great industrial center when Franklin Steele became the owner of riparian rights adjoining the Falls on the east bank where great flour mills now stand. Small grist mills appeared on both banks of the river and on Hennepin Island, that wooded barrier which pushed into the face of the Falls. Steele and others began construction of an A-shaped dam. The lower end of Nicollet Island gave up its growth of rock-maple and elm timber for dam logs.

Survey for logs.—Being afraid he might run out of logs, Mr. Steele sent

Logs in the River.

73

Bridge.

Daniel Stanchfield to explore the stretches of pine along the Rum River. Carrying heavy packs on their backs, Stanchfield and a companion waded swamps, climbed over fallen trees, met bears, wolves and other dangerous animals and fought flies and mosquitoes. They went clear to Mille Lacs, the source of the Rum River. Stanchfield reported to Steele that there was enough timber along the Rum River to last seventy-five years. Steele then made a deal with Stanchfield. Stanchfield was to go into the woods with crews and take out logs for Steele's mills. His salary was to be $50 a month and keep. Steele hired Ard Godfrey to run the St. Anthony mill for one-twentieth of what he made. R. P. Russel, a storekeeper, was to furnish food supplies for Steele's men. He charged $40 a barrel for beans, $2 a gallon for molasses, and $40 a barrel for pork.

Steele has many interests. — The Sibleys and the Steeles were very close friends since the wives were sisters. They went to each other's homes often.

As time went on Steele secured a site for the University and contributed towards the first building. Everyone was anxious to see a building started because they were afraid they would lose the right to the school if they didn't get some sort of a start.

In 1854 Mr. Steele leased a mill site on Hennepin Island to three other men who built a three-story flour mill. This was run by water from Steele's dam. They paid $200 a year for the water rights. This mill cost $16,000 and cleared $24,000 the first year.

Steele was one of the men who contracted for the first extension bridge across the Mississippi River. In 1857 he bought the Fort Snelling Reservation from the Government when they withdrew the troops. However, he could not keep up the heavy payments and when the Civil War started the Government took the Fort back again.

Though Franklin Steele was considered a wealthy man, he was involved in so many enterprises that he was always pressed for money. However, he was acknowledged to be one of the most active businessmen of his time.

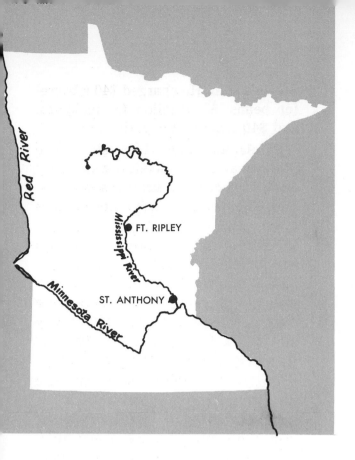

CHAPTER TWENTY-TWO

Anson Northrup

Builder . . . River Man

Anson Northrup came to Minnesota by ox cart from Illinois. He was one of the first settlers on the west side of the river where Minneapolis now stands. The first school was held in his house. Near it was a pond where the boys went swimming at recess. In front was a big swamp, full of cowslips and moccasin flowers.

Builds hotels. — Before coming to Minneapolis, Mr. Northrup had owned a hotel at Stillwater. It was famous for family dancing parties. In 1847 he had been part owner of the Oscola saw mill. In 1849 he built the American Hotel in St. Paul. In 1851 he built the St. Charles Hotel in Minneapolis on the east side of the river which was then called St. Anthony. This was one of the big, important

hotels of the time. In 1853 he built the Bushnell House in Minneapolis.

In the meantime he had been elected sheriff and his home was a popular place. Court was held there and it was a meeting place for the Masonic Lodge. By 1857 he was serving in the Legislature from Crow Wing County.

He goes into transportation. — In 1858 he owned the steamer North Star. He traded on the upper Mississippi to Fort Ripley. The next year the businessmen of St. Paul, wishing faster transportation than the Red River carts, offered $2000 to anyone who would first put a boat on the Red River and carry a cargo to Fort Garry where Winnipeg now stands.

Anson Northrup decided to win that money. He dismantled his boat, loaded the parts on sleds and wagons and started across country. It took 64 horses and 60 men to get it across the Territory because the hull was ninety feet long and twenty-four feet wide. They got lost on the prairie several times before they reached the Red River. Then they put the boat together again. He named it the "Anson Northrup." Someone broke a bottle of wine over its prow. It took him nine days to make the first trip. As soon as he proved to everyone that his boat could be used on the Red River, he sold it for $8000.

In 1862 he raised a company to defend the unprotected settlers of the frontier during the Indian massacres. Then he became a wagon master in the regular army.

Anson Northrup Steamer.

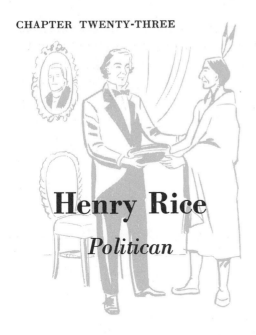

CHAPTER TWENTY-THREE

Henry Rice

Politican

Henry Rice came to Minnesota in 1839 at the age of 23. He was a tall, slender man who walked with a swaying motion. Before coming to St. Paul, he had been an agent for the American Fur Company. He became a neighbor and close friend of Governor Ramsey.

Booster for St. Paul. — From the very first, he boosted St. Paul. He said any village could become a city if it had a good harbor, good water power, or was located at the head of a river, or the junction of two navigable streams. Feeling sure St. Paul would grow, he got options on much of the land, buying some of it direct. He built stores, a warehouse, and a hotel called the American House which he put in charge of a woman named Mrs. Parker.

The very name of Rice stimulated investments. Within a month after it became the capital of Minnesota Territory, seventy new buildings were erected. The lumber was hauled from Stillwater or St. Anthony by ox teams.

Mr. Rice goes to Washington. — Henry Rice went to Washington as a delegate from Minnesota Territory. He helped with the new constitution. He did everything possible to advance the interests of the Territory. He had a great deal of power in Washington. He could go from the crude surroundings of a savage territory and enter into the Senate of the United States to command respect. Then he could return to the wilderness and command similar respect from Indian tribes. He pushed for pre-emption rights so people could buy up their claims for $1.25 an acre. He got postoffices for the new Territory. He got land offices and territorial roads. He got railroad grants from Congress.

Mr. Rice's personal endeavors. — During the time he worked for the good of the Territory, his personal activities were gaining wealth for him. By 1848 he owned eighty acres at seven corners which he had purchased for $400. It is worth millions today and netted him a big profit even then. That year he also owned a trading post near Sauk Rapids.

On Christmas of 1850 many Indians called on him to pay their respects. He gave each guest a loaf of bread. Bread was a sort of symbol to him since he was always pleading with the people of Minnesota to raise wheat. During those first days all the wheat was shipped into Minnesota for grinding into flour, instead of being shipped out as it is now. He kept repeating that Minnesota could become a great wheat center and this has since proved true.

He gave some of his land to churches when new ones were opened. He gave land for the first park in St. Paul.

His wife was a southern belle with a bright, beautiful face and black hair and eyes. She was much help to him in all his endeavors. Mrs. Rice, Mrs. Ramsey and Mrs. Neill were close friends.

St. Paul 1856.

CHAPTER TWENTY-FOUR

Father Lucian Galtier

Missionary

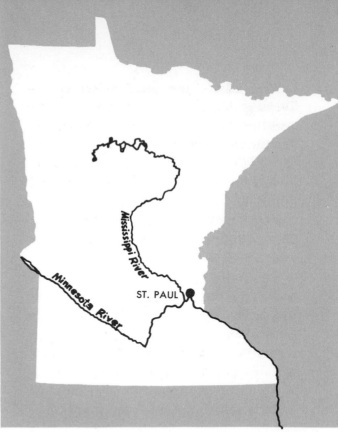

Father Lucian Galtier already knew something of the Sioux when he came to Fort Snelling charged with the duties of a wilderness priest.

There was no St. Paul then. There were no steamboats on the river. Only a few French Canadians lived at a place called "Pig's Eye," given in honor of a one-eyed pioneer who kept a shanty tavern. Then a band of Swiss, who had migrated from Canada to live near the Fort, were expelled from the Reservation. They sought homes farther down the river. Father Galtier felt sorry for the way they had been expelled from their homes. He knew how hard it was going to be for them to build new cabins and find places for their cattle to graze. He extended his care to them.

They start a church.—One of the Swiss donated a portion of his new claim for a church, a garden and a graveyard. At this place it was easy to cross the river and was the nearest point at the head of navigation. Eight of the men got together and erected a rude structure 25 by 18 feet.

It was built of oak logs, the rafters of tamarack from the swampy ground around it. The roof was of pine slabs brought from Stillwater in an ox cart. It was one story high with one door, four windows on either side and one in back.

New church is dedicated. — The little chapel stood among the trees and tangled growths with a simple cross topping the steep roof. It crowned the brow of what would some day be the city of St. Paul and could be seen for a long way. In November, 1841, it was solemnly dedicated to the service of God. Though it was almost as poor as the stable at Bethlehem, it became the nucleus of the city of St. Paul. It was blessed as the Chapel of St. Paul. Father Galtier did not want to use the name "Pig's Eye" and thinking so many other places like St. Croix, St. Peter and St. Anthony had been named for saints, decided him to use Paul. The chapel was no sooner topped with the cross then a trading house stood at its side. Traders always followed mission centers in search of gain. However, this hastened the progress of civilization because soon steamboats began to stop at St. Paul's landing.

Frequent trips made.—Father Galtier made frequent trips to other places to serve people without a church. He traveled by mackinaw boats or on foot. Since these places were in real wilderness without any comforts of civilization he often slept on the ground or in Indian tepees. He either went hungry or ate foods which he disliked. He was tormented by mosquitoes and had to cut his way through brush that left his clothing torn and his limbs bleeding.

Eventually Father Galtier was transferred to a parish at Keokuk, Iowa. He died in 1866.

Father Galtier's Church.

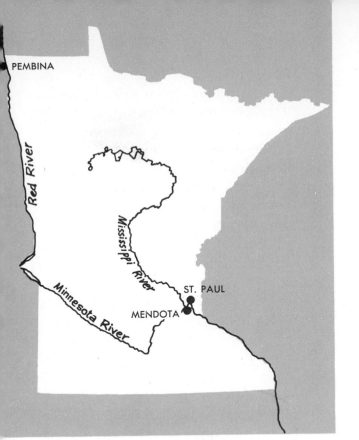

CHAPTER TWENTY-FIVE

Norman W. Kittson

Fur Trader . . . Legislator

From his trading post at Pembina near the Canadian border, Norman W. Kittson blazed a line of travel down the Red River Valley and across the territory to Mendota and St. Paul. For almost twenty years, the furs from Pembina were hauled in the curious, high-slung Red River carts, made entirely of wood, which could carry six hundred pounds each. They were pulled by oxen. The drivers walked lightly on moccasined feet, singing wildly to waken the quiet prairies. The distance of 448 miles from Pembina to St. Paul took about a month.

The drivers were half civilized, half barbaric, though very ingenious at their jobs. When the carts had to be taken across streams, as happened frequently, they removed the wheels from the carts and laid them on great buffalo robes made of many skins sewed together and then drawn up to form a canoe with the wheels making the bottom framework. One of these improvised canoes could float almost a thousand pounds across a stream.

81

Red River Cart Train.

Red River carts.—In 1844, Kittson ran only six carts. A few years later, there were 500 carts in a train. A freight train of today with 75 cars is very long. Then imagine what a train of 500 carts would be like, especially since they were never greased and squeaked so loudly they could be heard for hours before they reached St. Paul. If they were in dangerous territory, they made a great circle at night with the stock inside so as to be prepared against Indian attacks.

Leaving Pembina early in June, they reached St. Paul in July after following landmarks like Lac qui Parle, Swan Lake, Traverse des Sioux. They allowed four weeks in St. Paul and a wild time it was for both the drivers and the townspeople. Everyone wanted to buy the moccasins, mittens and gloves which the squaws from around Fort Garry had made because they were so brightly decorated with quills and beads and embroidery. Some of the men from Pembina brought along British sovereigns which they spent freely and as money was a scarce commodity, they were very welcome. They loaded up with tea, alcohol, hardware and clothing in exchange for furs, robes, pemmican and handwork. In August when they returned, the carts were almost as full as when they had come but the contents were quite different and eagerly awaited by the people at the northern post.

The business Kittson conducted as a partner for the American Fur Company was worth a quarter of a million dollars a year. A mink skin which brought 20 cents in 1857 was worth five dollars six years later.

Becomes public servant.—In 1850 Pembina got a postoffice and Mr. Kittson was made the postmaster. He had to have an assistant part time as he was soon elected a member of the Territorial Legislature. Although he was then known as Honorable Kittson, he traveled to St. Paul by dog team. One winter his wife was with him and died in St. Paul. They took her body clear back to Pembina by dog team to bury her.

Pembina was home to Kittson at that time. His trading post consisted of buildings around a great courtyard. The buildings were built of logs, mud-chinked. The trading post constituted an entire village with stores, a blacksmith shop, an icehouse and carpenter shop. The great courtyard was always crowded with half-breeds, Indians, horses, cattle and dogs. Towards the river were the barns, stables and hayracks.

After his wife died, Pembina didn't seem the same. He moved to St. Paul and became the mayor of the town. His interests still lay along the Red River and he established a steamship line on the river and became known as Commodore Kittson. After he had been in St. Paul awhile he no longer wore the leather clothing of the north. He became elegant in his dress and was very sprightly. He was a great friend of the Sibleys.

Later, he became a part of the corporation with Jim Hill to buy up defunct railroads.

Red River Cart.

CHAPTER TWENTY-SIX

Paul Bunyan

Legendary Logger

BEMIDJI

Land of Paul Bunyan

HACKENSACK

Mississippi River

When the early loggers gathered after a hard day in the woods, they loved to spin tales about Paul Bunyan. They told them so much that they began to believe they were real. They described him as the mightiest man who ever lived, so tall his head reached above the tallest tree. They said he had roamed all over northern Minnesota, performing feats unequalled by any other man. He decided to become a logger because he could cut down acres of trees with one swing of his axe.

The tales they told!—They claimed that when Paul Bunyan sneezed, the roof blew right off the bunkhouse. If he was outside when he sneezed and the day was frosty, the sneeze blew up a blizzard. They said all the men who worked for him had to wear earmuffs because his voice boomed so loud it could split their ear drums.

They declared he could tie an axe to the end of a rope and swing it around and it would cut all the timber it hit. He used a hollow tree for a horn to call the men together. Once he blew so hard a lot of trees fell down. He tried blowing toward the sky and raised a cyclone.

He used a whole tree for a fishing rod. His pipe was so big the tobacco had to be put in with a scoop shovel. His pipe smoked like a prairie fire.

It took such a big griddle to make flapjacks for Paul Bunyan that skaters tied slabs of bacon on their feet

Paul Bunyan and Ox.

and skated on the griddle to grease it. His doughnuts were so huge that three of them on a pole were all that two men could carry.

He could spin a log in the water so the bark would come off and then walk to shore on the bubbles. Mille Lacs was his bathtub.

When he wanted to sharpen an axe, he rolled a stone downhill and ran beside it, holding the axe against the stone.

He had trained big mosquitoes to dig his wells.

One winter the snow got so deep Paul had to dig down to find the tops of the tallest trees.

They claimed that Onion River got its name when the onions were so thick around there that Paul had to check the tears of his men while they cut down the trees.

He turned Dakota into a prairie by cutting down all the trees in one day.

Paul Bunyan was described as a colorful figure with a great red cap and yellow muffler. He wore a plaid mackinaw and bright green socks.

Paul Bunyan's Sweetheart.

His mittens were purple with white stripes.

The big blue ox.—His faithful helper was a big blue ox he called Babe. Babe ate a ton and a half of hay at a time. He could eat three wagonloads of turnips at once. His horns spread so wide that Paul could dry his clothes on them. His footsteps were so big that when water ran into them, it made lakes and that is how northern Minnesota got so may lakes.

Sometimes Babe wandered off and his tracks were so far apart that only Paul could follow him. If another man fell into one of those tracks, they had to toss him a rope before he could get out.

Babe is said to have hauled water from Lake Superior and he used the lake as a watering trough for himself. Once the tank in which he was carrying water from Lake Superior spilled over. That water made Lake Itasca and what ran off from it formed the Mississippi River.

It was no trick for Babe to haul a whole section of timber to the landing and he sledded whole farms out of the way.

Babe would only haul things when there was snow on the ground so Paul whitewashed all the roads to fool him.

When he found Babe needed shoes, he dug the iron ore to make them.

The symbol.—Paul Bunyan represents the romance of Minnesota's whispering pines and deep blue lakes. His great size and strength symbolized the spirit of ruggedness and adventure in God's great outdoors.

Bemidji claims to be the home of Paul Bunyan. The city has a steel statue eighteen feet tall of Paul and his blue ox. Be sure to see it when you go there.

Paul Bunyan had a sweetheart named Lucette Diana Kensack. You can see her statue at Hackensack.

CHAPTER TWENTY-SEVEN

Harriet Bishop

First Public Schoolteacher

When you attend school in Minnesota you are part of a great educational system which started back in 1847 when Harriet Bishop, our first Minnesota schoolteacher, came to St. Paul under the auspices of the Board of National Popular Education. Harriet Beecher Stowe had recommended her for the position.

Minnesota's first public school. — Though some attention had been given to the children at Fort Snelling, hers was the first real public school. It started in a log building with a bark roof and chinking of mud. It was only 10 by 12 feet and it had a stick chimney and a fireplace for heat. It had been a blacksmith shop. Its shaky door was hung on squeaky wooden hinges. Snakes crawled across the

path that led to the building. When Harriet went inside, rats scampered into holes in the corners.

She tacked cedar boughs over all the walls to cover the dirt and smells left by the blacksmith shop. She found an old pitcher without a handle and kept it filled with wild flowers which the children brought her. A man had been hired to drive pegs into the walls and lay boards across the pegs for seats. One board seat in the back of the room was reserved for visitors. A friendly hen refused to leave the place because she had a nest in one corner. Every day she came in to lay an egg.

They started with nine pupils and only two of them were whites. The others wore blankets. Even when the enrollment reached forty, only eight were pure whites. Dark faces were always peering in at the window. The Indians called the school "Good Book Woman's House."

Harriet Bishop taught the elementary branches and read the Bible to her pupils every day. In the evening she was apt to take walks up the hill to look out over the high bluffs along the river.

They work for a better building.—
As the enrollment grew, the need for a better building also grew. Harriet Bishop organized a sewing society to raise money for a new school. The new building would cost three hundred dollars but she told people it would also serve as a church, a place for elections and public assemblies and for court. It was to be 25 by 35 feet in size.

The sewing society raised only $25. When the officers at Fort Snelling heard about the project, they took up a collection and got $50 more. Others gave then. Although they didn't have quite enough the building went up anyway with hopes they would be able to pay off the debts later.

How the school was supported.—
Those first pupils had to pay for their schooling. It cost them about $3.00 a quarter. Fuel for the school was donated by the parents. Harriet brought school books with her as there were none to be bought in St. Paul until several years later.

The school system grew and Mr. Neill was the first State Superintendent. Minnesota has always had progressive men in that office.

Harriet Bishop becomes engaged.—
Harriet became engaged to marry a young lawyer in St. Paul. He had built them a little home and her trousseau was ready when his dominating older sister who had been East returned and forbade the marriage. The young man broke the engagement. This made Harriet very unhappy for a long time but eventually she married another man.

During the Civil War she was Mrs. McConkey, a volunteer worker in the St. Paul Aid Society. This Society worked for the good of the soldiers.

She was author of an historical book about the Indian Massacres. It was called "Dakota War Whoop." Before this, she had published a book called "Floral Home," where she recounted her pioneer experiences as a teacher.

CHAPTER TWENTY-EIGHT

Alexander Ramsey

First Governor

When you visit the handsome state capitol in St. Paul it is hard to realize that the first governor of Minnesota Territory lived in a hastily constructed frame house and managed the affairs of state from a hotel dining room. Yet no other governor lived through more terrifying times or left a greater impression on the State.

Arrival at St. Paul.—When Alexander Ramsey, a prince of a man, tall with heavy brows, dark eyes and broad shoulders, came to St. Paul in 1849, he brought his young bride with him. Since there was no place ready for them, they visited at the Sibley House in Mendota while a house was built. When they received word that the house was ready, Mr. Ramsey took his bride from Mendota to St.

Paul in a birch bark canoe. In those days the river was so clear they could see the bottom and it was a pleasure to float between the tree-covered banks. Mrs. Ramsey was so anxious to see their new house she could hardly wait.

When they climbed the hill from the dock and walked up the straggling street in St. Paul, some savages passed them with scalps dangling from their belts. Mrs. Ramsey clutched her husband's arm with a little shriek but more Indians were following. One had a red spot in the middle of his nose and one had a purple stripe where his hair was parted. The one back of him had black and yellow stripes across his forehead.

The young governor tried to lead his bride to the opposite side of the street but they had to stop to wait for a Red River car to pull through the mud. The whole town had only about a dozen frame houses and some log cabins.

The Governor goes to work.—They settled down in their crude home and the Governor began his official duties. He issued a proclamation declaring the Territory of Minnesota organized. About a week later, he issued another proclamation dividing the Territory into three judicial districts. Courts were to be held in Stillwater, St. Anthony and Mendota. You may think it strange that all the court business should be conducted in the small eastern section, but you must remember that was the only part which was settled at the time. To the west and north, the Terriory was a wilderness where savages roamed and hunted.

Of course, there was no building in which the new Territorial Council could meet so they gathered in a log tavern called "Bass' Tavern." Governor Ramsey ordered an immediate census of the Territory so people could elect delegates to Washington according to population. This census was to include only whites or people of mixed blood who were living in a civilized manner. The count showed there were only 4000 such people in the whole of Minnesota though it covered 166,000 acres, part of which is now in North and South Dakota.

The work of the Legislature.—Governor Ramsey held an election and Mr. Sibley was elected to represent Minnesota in the Congress of the United States at Washington. Our first Legislature met in the Central House Hotel with a flag outside to show that government business was being conducted. The opening prayer was given by Rev. Neill. Since they were meeting in the dining room, they had to adjourn when the boarders came to eat at noon.

Two sections of land were set aside in every township for schools. Right away speculators wanted to get hold of that land but Governor Ramsey stood firm, saying money derived from those lands could be used only for schools.

Of course, money was needed to conduct the affairs of the Territory so the Legislature levied taxes according to property valuations. Governor Ramsey urged that they pay as they went and not run into debt. He also urged that liquor traffic with the Indians be stopped since liquor made them absolutely unmanageable.

In other meetings the Legislature appropriated money for a State Historical Society. Up to that time history had been mostly of explorers and a few early settlers.

It was decided that since St. Paul got the capital, St. Anthony should have the University and Stillwater, the State Prison. They named Rev. Neill as superintendent of Education.

The State Seal.—With assistance, the Governor worked out a pattern for the Minnesota State Seal to be cut in metal. It was necessary to have such a seal since all state papers must be stamped with it. It showed a white man near St. Anthony Falls with a plow. A mounted Indian was riding towards the setting sun. The seal spoke the burning sentiment of the Territory. This sentiment was that the Indian must go when the white man came.

Knowing there would be trouble with the Indians, Governor Ramsey suggested that a military road be built from Fort Snelling to the Missouri River so that soldiers might be marched over the road once a year to show the might of the military. This was never done.

The Town Pump.—It is interesting to know that the town pump, which had a tall wooden framework, was used to post placards and notices. Thus, when people went to get water, they could get information at the same time.

The Indian question. — Governor Ramsey was a friendly man who talked freely with everyone. Some of his friends called him "Bluff Alec." He was being constantly reminded that the people of Minnesota must obtain the rich Sioux empire west of the Mississippi River so that new immigrants could find a place to settle without having their lives endangered.

In 1850 he met some Indians in a council at Fort Snelling and tried, as so many others had done, to make peace between the Sioux and the Chippewas who fought whenever they met. He told them the President of the United States was their Great Father and wanted them to till the soil and live like white men instead of roaming around and fighting.

Traverse des Sioux.—The biggest meeting between Indians and whites ever held in Minnesota occurred at Traverse des Sioux in 1851. This little trading post was on the Minnesota River, about where St. Peter now stands. It was on a wide, grassy prairie rising from the river bank. A few farming Indians had lodges set in the

Treaty at Traverse des Sioux.

middle of cornfields. There were some log buildings used by traders. There were the Mission buildings under the supervision of Rev. Hopkins. As a rule, the population at Traverse des Sioux was about thirty. It was really a gateway to the great fur country beyond.

Men who went to Traverse des Sioux.—Governor Ramsey and Luke Lea went down together. They were the government commissaries with orders to purchase all the land west of the Mississippi, claimed by the Sioux. Luke Lea's brother had been through the country with Nicollet on his explorations. His name was Albert and Albert Lea had been named

for him. Luke Lea had one wooden leg and walked with a limp but he was a Federal agent and a man of authority. They went on the boat named the "Excelsior." Other officials were on the same boat. There was Mr. Sibley from Mendota, Henry Rice from St. Paul, and Franklin Steele from St. Anthony. James Madison Goodhue came to report for the St. Paul paper. General Le Duc was there to report for the New York Tribune. There were reporters from other papers all over the country. There were clerks and secretaries and traders who hoped to collect money which the Indians owed them for goods they had advanced. Also there was Frank Mayer, an artist, who had come from the East to draw and paint pictures of the Indians.

Beside all the people, the boat was loaded with flour, rice, other food and baggage. They drove a whole herd of bawling cattle into the hold to be used for feeding the Indians while the meeting lasted. There was scarcely room to move around on the boat.

Messages to the Indians.—Couriers had been sent to every Indian camp, asking each tribe to come to the meeting because the United States wanted to buy all their land and would pay a good price for it. This land consisted of a territory almost as large as the State of Pennsylvania. It was the biggest land deal in Minnesota history. The whites had no qualms about getting this land from the redskins. They considered them wasters of good soil and nicknamed them "Red Republicans."

Camp at Traverse des Sioux.— As soon as the passengers got off the "Excelsior" at Traverse des Sioux, they found a cooking stove and table in one of the trader's log buildings and made use of them. A beef was killed and they had fresh steaks, pilot bread and vegetables. Rev. Hopkins from the Mission came to call and bid them welcome. He told them they could draw drinking water from his well.

They pitched tents along the shore. They put mattresses on the ground and each had a mosquito net to sleep under. They fought little biting gnats all day and in the evening they built smudges to keep mosquitoes away.

The Indians came in small numbers the first day so the waiting white men built a great arbor of aspen trees with a lattice top. Above it they raised the American flag.

The Indians begin to come. — On the third day a band of upper Sioux came in across the prairie with carts and ponies. They set up tepees. The next day a band of mounted Sissetons came. They formed a long line, singing wild war songs and beating drums as they advanced to present themselves to the Commissioners. Jumping off their ponies, they danced the Begging Dance, saying they were starving. They were given beef, rice, blankets and tobacco and rode off to set up a camp for themselves. After that, Indians kept dribbling in by cart and travois. They were only a small part of the number expected. One group brought along a young white wolf which was supposed to be tame but liked to jump at the horses, causing great confusion.

The Fourth of July. — They knew they would be there over the Fourth of July so the Commissioners named a committee to arrange a celebration. They planned that Rev. Hopkins should open with a prayer. After that there would be music by a band and the reading of the Declaration of Independence. Dinner was to be buffalo steaks, boiled ham, beef, vegetables and pastry.

Early that morning, Rev. Hopkins

went to the river to bathe. A short time later his clothes were found on the bank but he had disappeared and his body could not be found. Instead of a Fourth of July celebration, the whole day was spent in search of his body. It was not found for two days. The people whom he had served as a missionary were deeply grieved. One old squaw wept hysterically, though Indians seldom cry. The whole gathering was saddened by his death. There was a funeral the next day. Indians sang grief songs in Sioux. The white men conducted a service. He was buried where he had labored.

Prominent Chiefs arrive.—By that time many of the prominent chiefs had arrived with their bands. Little Crow from Kaposia came dressed in a white shirt, a bright neckerchief and an embroidered medicine bag

with buckskin trousers. His trousers and moccasins were brightly beaded and he wore a red belt. He dressed up so that Frank Mayer could paint his picture. For this he wore a tiara with weasel tails falling down behind and two small buffalo horns, one on either side. There was a crow totem on his back. He hid his deformed hands which he had gotten in a fight with his brother in a dispute over whom should be chief.

Red Iron who lived at Traverse des Sioux was a tall, athletic man who wore half-military and half-Indian clothing. He was a farming Indian who had a neat log cabin, barn and storehouse. Unlike the other Indians who passed the time in sleeping and playing games, he worked every day in his field, hoeing his corn and potatoes.

Sleepy Eye was there from Swan Lake and Chief Wabasha whose territory lay where Winona now stands.

While they waited. — For two weeks the Indians kept coming. The Commissioners could do nothing but wait. Governor Ramsey had to send back for more food. Laughingly they began to call it "The Reign of Beef." The Indians liked being fed. Every morning a delegate came from each camp for the food allotment. Butchers were kept busy slaughtering cattle and dividing the meat.

The Medicine Men set up a sort of hospital at Red Iron's farm. The sick were brought there and the Medicine Men tried to cure them, either by rattling gourds, shaking dried peas in a box or firing blank cartridges over their heads.

The big storm.—One night a terrific storm occurred. The men had to hold the tent poles down to keep their tents from blowing away. The canvas flapped wildly, water streamed down the sides and leaked in. Lightning came in red bolts and there were terrifying claps of thunder. In the morning when the sun came out and they could spread things out to dry, they found that even the keel boats had been driven from their moorings. That day they dug trenches around the tents to drain off the water. The Indians said the Thunder God had been growling at them. They claimed the Thunder Bird had dashed his wing on the river and broken open a fountain. They made little turtles of clay and prayed to them for good weather.

The good weather dance. — They prepared to give a dance to appease the Thunder God. They made a great circle on the prairie and raised a pole in the center. A bark image of the Thunder Bird was suspended from the pole. Nearby they built a little arbor of aspen boughs. Inside the arbor was an old Indian with blackened face and a grass wig on his head. He beat a drum to start the dancing and played a flute to stop it. Before the arbor was a bark image of a running buffalo, his legs stuck in the ground. Nearby was a red stone to represent the evil spirit.

The Indians danced around the arbor in a double hop. In another circle outside the dancers, the horsemen rode in blue embroidered blankets. They danced for some time. Then they shot down the Thunder Bird and the Buffalo. They said this would give them good weather.

The wedding.—The next day both whites and Indians attended the wedding of Nancy McClure and David Faribault. Nancy was a half-breed, fourteen-year-old girl who had been raised by her grandmother near Chief Red Iron's farm because her mother, who was dead, had been a cousin of the chief. She had studied in Rev. Hopkins' missionary school. She and her grandmother lived in a double tent with one for a sitting room and one for a kitchen. David was a half-breed boy about twenty. Everyone was invited to the wedding. The ceremony had to be performed by a justice since Rev. Hopkins was dead. The little bride had a white dress and slippers for the occasion but she trembled the whole time and would not lift her eyes. Afterwards the commissioners toasted the bride and groom with lemonade.

Entertainment.—The Indians took turns putting on entertainments. Little Crow and his braves put on a War Dance. Each carried a club, tomahawk or lance. They sang. At the end of each verse, a man went to the center of the circle and boasted of an exploit.

One evening some Indians covered

themselves with branches and mounted horses. Thus arrayed, they swept among the lodges of other bands in mock foray. They shouted when children darted out of the way and mothers screamed in fright. At each encampment they shot blank cartridges. In the end they all swept up in front of the Commissioner's bower, singing war songs.

There was always evening entertainment of some sort. Indians danced to drums made of hide stretched over kegs. Canadian voyageurs sang boat songs. The English remembered songs of Britain and the French added light musical airs. Sometimes the plaintive wails of bereaved wives or mothers, or the soft notes of a lover's flute carried on the night air.

The tribes play La Crosse. — The tribes spent one whole day playing La Crosse. Prizes were collected by carrying a pole from camp to camp for donations of belts, moccasins, saddles and wampum. The players were preparing by painting themselves and hanging sleigh bells around their necks. The judges were chiefs or old men.

La Crosse is much like football except the ball is smaller and is caught in the pocket at the end of a long stick, instead of in the hands. As the ball is thrown into the air, it is caught in the net and thrown or carried at great speed towards the other goal. At the end of the game, the victorious side receives the prizes which are divided among the players.

The gathering is complete.—After about two weeks thousands of Indians had gathered. Their tents spread out over the prairie in waves. Each camp was noisy with children and dogs. There was less than a hundred white men and yet they were always in command.

After many smaller conferences and meetings, the day for the actual signing arrived. It was the most imposing sight ever seen in Minnesota. All the dignitaries, headed by Governor Ramsey and Luke Lea, a large number of traders, the great Dakota chiefs in barbaric splendor with their painted followers behind them, the reporters and secretaries, were all gathered around the bower.

The secretaries and reporters stood at one side of Governor Ramsey's table. Traders and spectators sat on the ground. The chiefs had a semi-circle of benches. Thousands of Redmen congregated outside.

The offer. — Through translators, the Governor and Commissioner talked with the chiefs. They offered $30,000 in cash and the balance in yearly payments if the chiefs would relinquish their rights to Suland. They were promised reservations on which to live. The upper Sioux were to have a reservation extending ten miles on either side of the Minnesota River for a hundred miles. The lower Sioux were to have the same area on the lower river. They were to have schools, doctors, blacksmiths and all other artisans.

The Indians argued and argued. Sleepy Eye and Red Iron were opposed to signing. Finally they asked for another day to think it over.

By that time the food was almost gone and the leaves on the bower had turned brown and rattled in the wind. The Commissioners were getting desperate. However, because the deal was so big and of such tremendous importance to the whole territory, they had to grant another day.

On the sloping hillsides above Traverse des Sioux, tribal fires burned through the night. Flames etched prophetic designs on the dark faces of protesting warriors. In the curling wisps from ceremonial pipes, they made their decision to give up their lands to the United States Government though they knew it meant moving away from home villages and leaving the graves of loved ones to be buried again under growing fields.

When the Indians returned to the bower next morning, it was piled high with colored blankets, beads, ribbons, cloth, powder and lead which was to be presented to them when the signing was over.

One by one, the Indians stepped forward and made their marks except for Little Crow who had been to a Mission School and could sign his name. By signing, they ceded twenty-four million acres to the Federal Government at about twelve and one-half cents an acre. When the signing was completed, the gifts were presented,

the remaining supplies were divided among the chiefs and the white men with Governor Ramsey took the boat back to St. Paul.

Another treaty. — Shortly afterwards Renville guided Governor Ramsey with an escort of Dragoons from Fort Snelling to Pembina. Governor Ramsey stayed with Trader Norman Kittson while the Dragoons camped out on the prairie. Here the Governor made another treaty to obtain five million acres of land in the Red River Valley. Unknowingly, the Indians had signed away their heritages.

Settlements in Minnesota. — After that settlements in Minnesota increased at an amazing rate, especially along the Mississippi and Minnesota rivers. Sometimes whole colonies came from foreign countries or from the East and founded towns. In some places, people of one nationality came together. All of them brought saws and hammers and plows. They came to St. Paul in such numbers there was no place to stay and they had to camp in the streets. Mr. Sibley appointed a Board of Immigration. The influx of settlers spurred the lumber industry since there was need for so many new homes and business places.

Governor Ramsey makes the first payment.—In November of the next year Governor Ramsey went by team to Traverse des Sioux to make the first land payments as had been promised in the treaty. He carried $275,000 in cash. Mr. Sibley went with him

Central House in St. Paul.

and Joseph R. Brown went along as interpreter.

The first Capitol.—The first Capitol buildings was completed in 1853. Candles furnished lights for the evening meetings. The room where the legislature met was heated by four box stoves.

The Civil War touches Minnesota.—Governor Ramsey was in Washington, D. C., on business when the Civil War was declared. He went at once to President Lincoln and offered one thousand men from Minnesota.

The Sioux massacres.—Because of the Civil War and other reasons, the Indians who had been moved to reservations did not get their annuities on time. They were without food and necessary clothing and in resentment they broke out with violent massacres, killing people and animals and taking many prisoners. Ramsey appointed Mr. Sibley to head an army to subdue them. If you read the story of Mr. Sibley, you will learn what he did at that time.

Mr. Ramsey served the State for half a century. His name is carried in many places. Two of them are Ramsey County and Ramsey State Park.

Present Capital of Minnesota at St. Paul.

CHAPTER TWENTY-NINE

Edward Duffield Neill

Preacher . . . Educator

Anyone who lives in Minnesota knows about our wonderful school system but few know that the first Superintendent of Public Instruction in Territorial days was a Presbyterian minister named Edward Duffield Neill.

Mr. Neill and his wife came to the village of St. Paul in 1849. He was to serve as a Presbyterian minister. He was a tall, light-haired man with side whiskers. He walked lightly as if there were springs on his feet. As they climbed the steep hill from the boat landing, a chief in a red blanket and decorated leggings with his face painted in many colors, passed them. He carried a gun, a hatchet and a pipe. Behind him walked a squaw with a papoose on her back. Its little head stuck out the top, dangling like it might break.

Mrs. Neill was ready to go back home. Mr. Rice walked up to them and introduced himself. When he saw how disappointed she was in the town, he put a broom over his shoulder and led a march to the American House, the best hotel in town. Mrs. Neill laughed so hard at his antics that she forgot to be frightened.

The American House.—The American House was a new building and the floors were so full of splinters they could not remove their shoes until they were ready to get into bed or they might get slivers in their feet. It was a noisy place for it was from there that the stages left for other towns. Balls and dinner parties were given, people gathered for social intercourse and many real estate deals were made over the tables in the dining room.

The only furniture in Neill's room was a bed and a wash-stand. Rev. Neill wrote his first sermon on the little stand, setting the bowl and pitcher on the floor while he wrote. A brick house was being built for them and they had brought their furniture along for the house. This was stored in a shed while they waited. Mrs. Neill wanted to put one of her carpets on the bedroom floor at the hotel and add a few pieces of her own furniture to make the room more comfortable. The landlady would not permit it.

They move into the chapel. — The members had started building a chapel for Mr. Neill and that was finished before their home. Mr. and Mrs. Neill moved into the chapel and lived there for six weeks. On Sunday they had to take down the bed for services.

Everyone had a storehouse then because they had to buy in large quantities. Mr. Neill had bought a side of beef, frozen it and put it in his storehouse. The next Sunday, in his sermon, he said that anyone in need should come to him. That night someone stole all the beef out of the storehouse.

How they made friends. — Mrs. Neill and Mrs. Ramsey were both brides, both new in a strange country and became good friends. They exchanged recipes and ideas and entertained together.

Someone left a big bag of supplies on Neill's doorstep the day before Christmas. They never did find out

Behind him walked a squaw with a papoose on her back.

who left the welcome gift.

The first Thanksgiving was celebrated by order of Governor Ramsey on December 26, 1850. The Protestants all gathered to hear a sermon by Mr. Neill. In this sermon Rev. Neill made the following prophecy. "Is there not a prospect that in half a century, the Indian lodges that now surround us will be far removed, that the shores of Lake Pepin will be strengthened by the religion of Christ, that steam engines will carry produce across the country, that mission stations will be replaced by white school houses, church spires and seminars of higher learning?"

Mr. Neill becomes a leader.—When the Neills moved into their new brick house they were neighbors to the Ramseys. Governor Ramsey and Mr. Neill discussed the problems of the Territory together. When the school question came up in the Legislature, Rev. Neill was made the first Superintendent of Public Instruction. The new government formed a State Historical Society also and Mr. Neill made the first address to that organization. He helped publish the first Dakota directory, was the author of the first Teacher's Register and wrote books about Minnesota's beginnings, getting his material from old documents which were presented to the State Historical Society.

In 1858 he was made a Chancellor for the new State University. He was always ready to advance educational interests.

When the Civil War came, he was made a chaplain for the first troops and went with them to war. Years later he came back to act as president of Macalester College.

Lower Levee and Wabasha Street Bridge.

CHAPTER THIRTY

James Henry Goodhue

Editor

No sooner had Minnesota been proclaimed a territory than James Goodhue arrived in St. Paul to start a four-page newspaper called the Pioneer. He was a bold, energetic young man, unafraid to tackle the difficulties of starting a newspaper in a new country. Although he was a graduate of Amherst College, he was able to live in a shack and overcome tough situations.

His first newspaper office certainly offered no comfort, for light and wind came in through a thousand cracks between the logs. However, he boosted Minnesota from the first moment he arrived. He stated that the Territory would soon be a great farming country with fields of grain everywhere.

Advice to emigrants.—He advised emigrants to bring along tents and bedding since building could not keep up with the demand for homes. He promised them the climate would be so wonderful that living in a tent would be a pleasure. He promised

that Minnesota would soon have railroads. He said the railroad should follow the trail of the Red River, across to the Columbia Basin between Washington and Oregon, over which the mails were being carried by the American Fur Company.

Soon after arriving he built a small house for his family. This he later turned into a printing shop and bought a better home.

He had a vivid imagination and when cold weather came and he was so uncomfortable in his poorly heated shop, he wrote that cold weather could not freeze warm hearts.

Opposes the schemers.—Almost at once he ran into trouble with the scheming element of the town who only wanted to make money without regard to others. He had no mercy on them, exposing them in his editorials. He stood for virtue and honesty and let everyone know it, even refusing to run advertisements that were not strictly honest.

The cranberry harvest.—In December he reported three thousand barrels of cranberries had been shipped from St. Paul and Mendota and almost half that amount from Stillwater. He claimed that Minnesota berries were twice as large and twice as delicious as those from the East. At that time the cranberries sold for $4 a barrel. They were gathered by the Indians who took them into town to exchange for goods. Farmer's children also picked and often cranberries could be found right in the bogs and marshes around St. Paul.

Social life in St. Paul—Goodhue was not able to speak of any other exports from St. Paul that year but he did emphasize the fact that it had a rich social life. He reported how calls were exchanged on New Year's Day with people wrapped in furs going from place to place in sleighs and cutters. He reported how everyone attended the ball at the Central House in the evening.

Advice to city officials.—He urged that the city officials make the river bank into a boulevard so buildings would not be erected to mar its beauty for passing boats.

The treaty at Traverse des Sioux.—When the Governor and most of the other celebrities of the day went to Traverse des Sioux to attend the big Indian conference where the Sioux sold millions of acres to the Federal government, Goodhue went along to report for his paper. The Indians held out so long that he couldn't stay for the finish but made arrange-

Corner of Wabasha and Fourth Street, St. Paul, in 185

ments with a reporter from New York to send him the late news from Traverse des Sioux. When the treaty was finally signed, he wrote that it was a pillar of fire, lighting the way to a promised land. He added that farms with fences, waving wheat fields and rustling maize, cities with white cottages and tall buildings and railroads would soon spread over the land.

Goodhue had a wife who could help him with the paper in an emergency. The emergency came when he published an editorial about a judge who frequently absented himself from duty. He called the judge several unsavory names. Later he met the judge's brother on the street and they fought; both men were injured and laid up for awhile.

This practically ended his career as an editor. He died shortly after while still a very young man. If he had lived, no doubt he would have followed a wonderful career in Minnesota for he wrote with an inspired pen.

CHAPTER THIRTY-ONE

Little Crow
Indian Chief

Little Crow became chief of the Kaposia band near the pre-destined city of St. Paul when his father died. When death was near, Little Crow's father called for Sibley who was his friend. In Sibley's presence he told his son that he had been a bad boy. He asked him to listen to Sibley's advice and follow his direction. Almost his last words to Little Crow were, "Do not quarrel with the Whites."

Little Crow succeeded his father as chief but he was a lazy, arrogant man. He had several wives and all of them were sisters. Though everyone knew him to be a liar, he was really devoted to his children, especially his oldest son. When the boy was only fourteen, Little Crow took him to every Council in embroidered garments with silver medals around his neck. When Little Crow was urged to cut his hair and dress like a white man he refused, although he did sometimes wear trousers and shirts instead of blankets.

The Indian massacres.—In 1862 he led the Sioux against the Whites, killing and robbing people wherever they went. He fought against the Whites at New Ulm and endeavored to wipe out the town which was saved by Judge Flandrau.

He attacked Fort Ridgley, a military post on the Minnesota River. They fought him off there but he took many captives when he retreated.

The Governor put Mr. Sibley in charge of an army to go against Little Crow. Sibley hated to do this because they had hunted and fished together. He sent notes to Little Crow, asking him to surrender. Little Crow pleaded forgiveness on the strength of their past friendship. Sibley refused and ordered Little Crow to give up. Little Crow fled, leaving his people to be taken by the Whites. At Camp Release Sibley collected many prisoners whom Little Crow had taken. It was said that Little Crow had at first opposed the massacres but after they started he became as bloodthirsty as any of the others.

Little Crow escapes.—The government rounded up the culprits and many of them were hanged for their crimes. Little Crow could not be found. However, he was accidentally shot later when he was picking berries near Hutchinson.

His picture can still be seen.—Long before the massacres when Little Crow attended the big Council at Traverse des Sioux, his picture was painted with a headdress trimmed with beadwork and weasel tails and buffalo horns on either side. This picture can be seen at the Minnesota Historical Society and in many books.

Little Crow lived near the pre-destined city of St. Paul.

CHAPTER THIRTY-TWO

Colonel John H. Stevens

Father of Minneapolis

In Minnehaha Park, Minneapolis, stands the first house built on the west side of the Mississippi River in that city. It was hauled from its original place by the river, by the school children of Minneapolis because this little house saw so much of the law-making of the early territory.

Colonel John H. Stevens came to Fort Snelling to work for Franklin Steele who was the sutler, or storekeeper, at the Fort. Colonel Stevens, who had earned this title in the Mexican War, worked as a bookkeeper and post office clerk.

Assigned land. — Many wanted to settle on the Fort Snelling Reservation, feeling that it included much more land than it should. However, this was not allowed. Nevertheless, the War Department loaned Colonel Stevens 160 acres of land across the river from St. Anthony if he would run the ferry across the river to transport government troops and supplies.

Builds a house.—Although he had no title to the land, Colonel Stevens built a house with windows facing the river where the big Union Depot now stands. He planted lilacs about the house. A slope led up to a patch of rolling prairie where oak trees furnished acorns for the squirrels that scampered around the tepees of the band of Indians that camped there in summer. This place is now called Bridge Square. Winding down to the river was the road where they hauled up water with a flat cart holding barrels. Stretching far back from the house there was only wilderness which is now the city of Minneapolis. In the wilderness were wild plums and cherries.

Colonel Stevens plants.—Knowing

that emigrants thought Minnesota was a barren place, Mr. Stevens plowed up a large area and planted corn, wheat and oats. Everything came up, proving that grain could be successfully raised in Minnesota. He introduced the first herd of cows also and they thrived. Before that, no one had kept cows except at the Fort.

Fighting off mosquitoes, he made a big garden back of his house. The Indians thought it was all right for them to come down from their settlement and help themselves to his vegetables so he made a deal with them. They were very fond of crackers and salt pork so he kept a barrel of each on hand. Whenever they came to his home he gave them some if they promised to leave his garden untouched. They agreed to this. When fall came they brought him game but they expected to be paid for it.

How the Stevens' family lived.— You may think the Stevens' family led a dull life with only roaming Indians for neighbors and mail coming only once a week from Fort Snelling. This was not the case, however. Mrs. Stevens had a piano and was a very good musician. They subscribed to a number of magazines from the East. Although they had no church, Gideon Pond often came to hold services in

Minneapolis in Colonel Steven's time.

their home and others came to hear him.

St. Anthony grows. — Across the river they could see a village growing, the village of St. Anthony. First it was a few log houses. People from those cabins began to come across the ferry to the west side where the Stevens lived. Some of them liked the west side so well they even asked if they could build on Stevens' land. Of course, it was not really Colonel Stevens' land but belonged to Fort Snelling and was forbidden territory as far as settlers were concerned.

Then a bill was passed in Congress reducing the size of the Fort Snelling Reservation. That left Colonel Snelling's land outside the military territory. However, there were no provisions for him to buy the land. It still belonged to the Government and he had no deed for it.

His land surveyed. — People wanted to come there so badly that Colonel Stevens employed a surveyor named Charles Christian to survey 100 acres of his land and lay out a town site. He, himself, decided on the width and direction of the streets and the size of the lots. One of the streets ran parallel with the river and was named Washington Avenue. This name was given by a woman named Elizabeth Daly, a vest maker who had come from Brooklyn. Elizabeth was so lonesome for Washington Avenue in Brooklyn that Colonel Stevens told her to call the avenue "Washington" so she would feel at home. With a

hot poker she burned the name Washington Avenue on a board. She nailed the board to a tree and the name stuck.

To streets running at right angles to Washington Avenue, Colonel Stevens gave the names of Hennepin for Father Hennepin and Nicollet for the French explorer. Today this is the business section of Minneapolis and is worth millions of dollars.

The Colonel gives away lots. — Then the Colonel actually offered to give lots to anyone who would erect a building worth at least three hundred dollars. Almost at once, he had the beginning of a city since the first lots were used for business establishments such as dry goods and hardware stores. There was a blacksmith shop, a carriage factory and a livery stable. These were followed by a lumberyard and shops for millinery and tailoring. Added to that were a dressmaker's establishment, an insurance office, a bookstore, a gun and harness shop, a land office and a post office.

The Claim Jumper's Association. — Of course, they had no title to all this land and could give none. Consequently, the Colonel himself, as well as the new settlers and businessmen, lived in constant fear of losing their homes and establishments. Meeting at Stevens' home, they formed what they called a Claim Jumper's Association to protect themselves if anyone tried to take their places. You may be sure they were all relieved

Some of the first homes in Minneapolis.

when the government granted what they called "pre - emption rights," which meant that all who had claims could buy them up at $1.25 an acre.

Colonel Stevens' home becomes a public center.—Colonel Stevens immediately paid for his claim and received a clear title. Then he gave deeds to all the homeowners on his land and everyone felt better. By this time his home had become a meeting place for almost every organization in the area. When they wanted a name for the new town, they met at the Stevens' home and after much argument decided on the name of Minneapolis.

United States Judges of Federal Court used the Stevens' parlor to decide questions of law. Missionaries held meetings there. Preachers of various faiths converted their listeners and then took them down to the river to baptize them. Visitors and tourists were always invited to stay at their home. One famous visitor was Fredericka Bremer, a Swedish au-

thoress, who later wrote an account of her travels in Minnesota.

Even the Indians held meetings at Stevens' home to consult with government agents. Little Crow, Good Road, Gray Eagle and Shakopee were some of the chiefs who met there. Here also was organized the first agricultural society, the first singing school, the first lyceum. Colonel Stevens was made a trustee at the first school election. He helped oversee the building of the first school where the Courthouse now stands.

After the most pressing problems of the new city were settled, Colonel Stevens was approached by a group of men who wanted to take up claims in an agricultural section. Since most of the claims around Minneapolis had been taken, Colonel Stevens with Norman McLeod as guide, took the group on a tour of inspection for good claim land. They decided on the place which later became Glencoe. Each member of the party selected a claim and they platted out the new village.

109

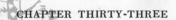

CHAPTER THIRTY-THREE

Joe Rolette

Fur Trader . . . Legislator

Rolette in Voyageur Costume.

When you visit Pembina in the northwestern corner of Minnesota, you may see a memorial in the State Historical Park, dedicated to Joseph Rolette. This is a cairn with a bronze plate bearing the name, "King Rolette."

In 1849 when Minnesota became a Territory, Joseph Rolette was a leading citizen of Pembina on the Red River near the Canadian border. Although he had received some education for the priesthood, he was known up and down the river as a fur trader. Every trapper within miles came to his post at least once a year to bring in their furs and get goods in exchange.

Rolette's cart brigade.—He had a cart brigade that worked between Pembina and St. Paul. As many as 125 carts were in one brigade. They carried great loads of furs to St. Paul and Mendota and brought supplies back to the people of the north. The carts were made of wood and looked like big box crates, set between two gigantic wheels. They were pulled by oxen harnessed with rawhide straps. Such a cart cost $15 and lasted three trips. It held up to 700 pounds and followed natural prairie roads in company with the rest of the train.

Joe Rolette as a man.—Joe Rolette was the sort of man who would dash right into a herd of buffalo and shoot his way out. He was admired for his great daring. So it was quite natural when the Territory of Minnesota was organized that Joe Rolette should be sent to the Legislature as a representative from the north. He came driving into St. Paul in a cariole drawn by three big Eskimo dogs, the bells on their harness tinkling and flashing in the sun. He was all dressed up in voyageur clothing, leather suit, a fire bag and moccasins. He created quite a sensation when he dashed into the capital city. He didn't mind that at all. He'd created a similar stir when he went to New York for a short time to attend school and appeared in leather clothing.

At St. Paul he brought the dogs right into the Council Chambers. Everyone petted them and fed them. He laughed and said the animals weren't used to such treatment. On the trail they'd received only a pound of pemmican each night. He'd bought the pemmican at trading places along the way. It was made of buffalo meat, pounded into shreds and stuffed into hide bags, sealed with hot tallow which hardened as it cooled. He told them pemmican was just as good for man as it was for beast. He used it often for himself when he was on the trail. He told them it had taken him sixteen days to reach St. Paul.

Excusing himself, he went to meet Governor Ramsey. He was still dressed in leather clothing with his fire bag dangling in front. His black hair hung in long curling waves.

Joe Rolette pulls a trick.—Because of his merry nature and magnetic personality, he was very influential in the Legislature. He was given the nickname of "Jolly Joe."

In 1857 when a bill was introduced to move the Capitol from St. Paul to St. Peter, Joe Rolette was on the enrolling committee. The fate of the bill rested on this committee. Naturally the people of St. Paul did not want to lose the Capital. Neither did Joe Rolette. He had interests in St. Paul and St. Peter was a long way from Pembina.

Joe Rolette just disappeared. The other members waited and had people searching for him. The members did not even adjourn but had cots put up by their desks and ate and slept there. They could not pass the bill without a two-thirds vote and that meant Joe Rolette had to be there. Finally it came time to adjourn and they had to break up without a vote. That automatically killed the bill.

Later it was revealed that Mr. Rolette had put the bill in a safe at the Fuller House and kept himself hidden in the hotel until the time had passed. Of course, he became quite a hero in St. Paul because he had saved the capital for that city. The people of St. Peter did not really appreciate what he had done. However, St. Paul has been the capital ever since.

CHAPTER THIRTY-FOUR

Charles
Eugene Flandreau

Indian Agent . . . Jurist
Soldier

If you have ever been to New Ulm, perhaps you saw the bronze shaft with a relief of Colonel Charles Flandreau who became a hero when he defended the town against the Indian raids during the Sioux uprising.

Charles Flandreau was tall, dark-haired and active. He came to St. Paul as a young man and was there on New Year's Day. It was the custom to go calling on that day. With other young men, he made 150 calls and was fed everywhere he went.

Mr. Flandreau at New Ulm. — In 1855 he was a deputy clerk of court in the German settlement which had been started at New Ulm. The Germans had laid out an immense tract of land, covering thousands of acres in the land of freedom. Most of them had come from overseas to join the colony.

After a claim was chosen, the head of the family had to go to Winona to enter his land in the courthouse. They had to go by steamboat and most of them could not talk English. They did not understand our laws either. Mr. Flandreau took them in groups of 40 to 50 at a time to sign up for their homesteads.

They came to him with every difficulty. When they wanted a post office, they asked him. He wrote to Honorable Henry Rice in Washington and soon New Ulm had a post office. Mr. Flandreau saw to it that each family signed naturalization papers so they would be eligible for preemption of the land. This meant that after they met the requirements, they could buy their claims from the government for $1.25 an acre. They loved him so much they often called him "The Plumed Knight of the Border."

An Indian agent.—In 1856 he was appointed Indian agent for the Sioux. He had charge of one agency at Redwood and another at Yellow Medicine. When he was with the Indians he dressed in buckskin as they did. He was so tanned from being outdoors, that sometimes it was hard to tell him from the redmen.

New Year's Day at Yellow Medicine.—He was at Yellow Medicine over New Year's Day. He knew the squaws called it "Kissing Day" and for each kiss they expected a gift. He had several barrels of gingerbread baked and bought whole bolts of calico which he had cut into dress lengths. Forty-eight squaws called on him that day. Each one kissed him, accepted the gifts of calico and gingerbread and left. They called him "Ay-tah" which meant father.

Legislator and Justice. — He held another position as a member of the Territorial Legislature at that time also. In 1857 he helped frame a state constitution.

Fort Ridgley.

He was appointed to the very important position of Justice of the Supreme Court. He moved to Traverse des Sioux then. The courts and law offices were widely scattered and he generally walked from place to place. He thought nothing of walking seventy-five miles.

The Sioux massacres.—One day a courier came to his home at four o'clock in the morning. The man had ridden so fast his horse was shaking and lathered with sweat. He told Judge Flandreau that the Sioux were killing the settlers on the frontier, especially around New Ulm. They wanted Mr. Flandreau to come to their rescue just as he had done countless times before. He told the man he would come right away.

Judge Flandreau sent his wife and baby to St. Paul where they would be out of danger. Then he made a plea for troops. One hundred and sixteen men responded. They elected him as their captain.

He sent eighteen mounted men ahead to New Ulm to tell them help was on the way. They told afterwards how they dashed into the town at full gallop even while the Indians were attacking.

Judge Flandreau arrived with the rest of his men that evening. They got into the town and you can imagine the joy of these poor, besieged people who had been fighting off fire and arrows for two days. They thought Judge Flandreau could do anything and they felt sure he would save them.

Mr. Flandreau organizes a military staff.—Judge Flandreau found there were more than 1500 defenseless women and children in the community. He organized a military staff. He sent out 150 men to bring in refugees and bury the dead. They managed to get out of town but the Indians kept riding around New Ulm, hoping to starve the people out. Flandreau gathered all the people into the center of the town so the empty outside buildings served as barricades. As soon as news of the attack spread, more help came to them from other communities.

Flandreau moves to Mankato. — After they had chased the Indians out onto the prairie, Flandreau rounded up 150 wagons. They took more than 1500 scared, sick and wounded women and children clear across to Mankato, thirty miles away. Men with guns rode beside the wagons. They expected every minute to be attacked but they got through safely. The people of Mankato took them all in and cared for them although the town would hardly hold them all. The massacres continued for some time. Plows were left in the furrows, churches became hospitals, homes were deserted.

He continues to serve. — In 1867, Mr. Flandreau moved to Minneapolis where he became city attorney. In 1890, he came out of retirement to help frame a new charter for St. Paul.

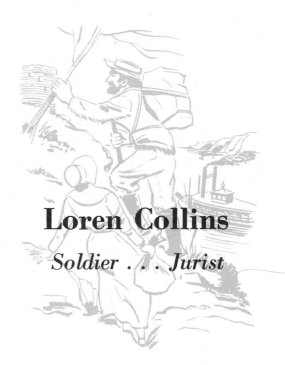

CHAPTER THIRTY-FIVE

Loren Collins

Soldier . . . Jurist

People who live around St. Cloud still remember the name of Loren Collins as a prominent citizen and a Supreme Court Judge. His life was a good example of how a poor but enterprising boy can attain success.

Collins comes to Minnesota. — He was just a lad when he came from the East with his family in 1854. Steamboat business was big that year and fifteen other boats were unloading at the St. Paul levee when they got off the boat that had brought them upstream. Young Collins noticed that the boats returned south again almost empty since Minnesota

hadn't started shipping wheat and other products as they do now. In fact, they even had wheat shipped in to make bread.

While his father went to buy supplies to keep them going on a claim at Eden Prairie which he had staked out on a previous trip, the rest of the family walked about to inspect St. Paul. Young Collins remembered for years after how the sounds of saws and hammers were everywhere because St. Paul was building so fast. And he was also attracted to the newly trimmed cupola on the Territorial Capitol Building.

Scene at Fort Snelling.

Excitement at Fort Snelling. — By the next day they were ready to take another boat to Fort Snelling with cattle, flour, feed and all the other supplies their father had bought. They had to unload at Snelling to go across country. The hill from the dock to the Fort was very steep. They got the cattle up and part of their provi-

First Capital Built in 1853.

sions. Then young Loren was assigned to watch the cattle while his father went down to bring up some more of their things. One white heifer was very wild and Loren tied her to a wagon wheel which wasn't fastened securely. The heifer got frightened, pulled off the wheel, and boy, wheel and cow all tumbled down the hill together. You can imagine all the excitement. Soldiers came running from the Fort and got them safely up the hill again.

They go to Eden Prairie. — Finally everything was packed in their three wagons with a team of oxen hitched to each wagon. They had ten head of cattle and some pigs to drive ahead of them. It took them a couple of days to reach their claim. By that time most of their money was gone, but they had a little corn and oat seed and plenty of garden seeds which they had brought from the East. They also had a good supply of potatoes which they planted and the boys planted watermelon seeds. They made log fences to keep the cattle in and log pens for the pigs.

That first year they lived on potatoes, corn, beans and game which they caught. They had to haul all their water from the lake a half mile from the house.

When the corn reached the milk stage in its growing, the blackbirds swarmed all over the field, picking the ears open. The boys had to stay in the fields all the time to chase them away. By fall the potato crop was so big they had to dig a hole in the side of the hill to keep them. They got tired of digging potatoes, but next spring their father made enough off them to buy a team of horses.

On the road to Shakopee. — They were near the road which led to the Indian village of Shakopee. A short distance from their farm was a red stone where the Indians always gathered to go through some sort of a religious ritual. Loren and his brothers got to know most of them and were friendly with the Indian boys.

They sell their watermelons.—The boys got such a big crop of watermelons that they took a load to St. Anthony and sold them to the mill workers. It took them three days to make the trip back and forth but they each earned $10 and that seemed like a lot of money to them.

When Loren was old enough he took up a claim for himself but he had been on it only a short time when a terrific storm wrecked all his buildings and great hail stones flattened everything. He went to Kenyon and there he met a lawyer who suggested he give up farming and study law instead. He decided that was what he wanted to do and in later years when he became a judge, he always said that a hail storm made a lawyer out of him.

Loren decides to become a lawyer. —He had no money to start his studies so he got a job teaching a country school. He boarded around with the various families and when the four-month term was over he received $60 for the time he had been there. He took this money and went to Hastings to study law with a firm in that city. He had to earn his way as he studied by doing extra jobs.

In the Civil War.—The Civil War began and he enlisted. Soon he made the grade of Second Lieutenant. When the Sioux outbreak occurred his regiment was ordered to the border. He was in the Battle of Wood Lake and helped free the prisoners which the Indians were holding at Camp Release.

He came out of the service as a Post Adjutant and was admitted to the bar soon afterwards. Soldiering had given him good training for legal work. He had been fearless in battle and received constant promotions. And he had been genial with all his associates.

He practices at St. Cloud. — He went to St. Cloud to practice law. At the same time, he filled many other positions. He was mayor of the city for four terms. He was the county attorney for four terms and a state representative for two terms. In 1883 he was appointed a District Judge. Four years later he was an Associate Judge of the Supreme Court. He held this elevated position for seventeen years. His clients had great faith in his judgment and respected his opinions.

He died in 1912.

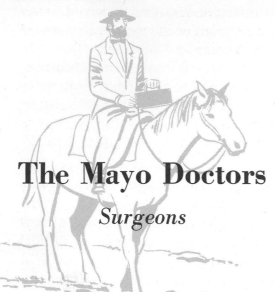

CHAPTER THIRTY-SIX

The Mayo Doctors

Surgeons

If you have ever been to Rochester you have seen the 22-story Mayo building towering over the city. You probably learned that it has every facility for medical diagnosis and is world famous.

William Mayo came to southern Minnesota by way of St. Paul when that city had only a few thousand people. For several years he practiced around Le Sueur, walking over weedy trails, carrying a tin lantern at night. Sometimes he rode horseback. When he came to a stream, he crossed by canoe or boat. He went to log cabins, old shacks and even to tents to treat people. Most of them were so poor they could not pay him. Often they gave him a chicken or a few vegetables for his services. Sometimes they asked him to treat their animals.

The move to Rochester.—The Civil War had started when Dr. Mayo moved to Rochester. He got a job on the enrollment board. He examined volunteers and later, draftees. Then he went into private practice. About that time the railroad reached Rochester. He became a familiar figure in his long-tailed, double-breasted coat and top hat. He carried an air of prosperity but he was not prosperous. He mortgaged his home to buy a $600 microscope and it took him ten years to pay for it.

His two sons. — Doctor Mayo and his wife had two sons growing up. Will was a slender blonde boy.

Dr. Mayo and his sons.

Charles was short, dark and stocky. Doctor Mayo moved to a farm so he could have horses and so the boys could keep busy. Charles loved the farm. Will hated it. Yet both had their work to do. They cared for the horses and took turns driving the doctor out on country cases.

St. Mary's Hospital.

Though he hired a man to do the actual farm labor, he managed it along with his medical duties. He also took an interest in civic affairs at Rochester. He served on the school-board, brought lecturing celebrities to town, and took the initiative in starting a public library.

His medical career. — Dr. Mayo practiced all forms of medicine but he most wanted to be a surgeon. Often he had to depend on his common sense to tell what was wrong with a patient. If surgery was necessary, he operated right in the patient's home, often on the kitchen table. He used surgical tools made by the black-smith.

When the boys were small, he took them on cases and let them watch. They began to learn to roll bandages and use a microscope. They helped make plaster casts. They cut thread to tie blood vessels. They sterilized his instruments. And they met many medical men of the time who chanced to stop over at Rochester.

Being raised in a medical tradition, it was quite natural that both boys should decide to study the subject. They went to college and studied to follow in their father's footsteps.

The big storm.—Doctor Mayo had been in Rochester for twenty years when the city was struck by a terrible tornado. Lower Town was almost demolished. By that time, young Will and Charles were doctors and Will established headquarters at Buck Hotel in Lower Town. Doctor Will and Charles teamed up at the Mayo office. So many had been hurt that they treated scores of people.

Rochester needed a hospital. — It was decided that Rochester needed a hospital. The Sisters of St. Francis began collecting funds for St. Mary's Hospital. When it became evident that the hospital was really to be built, Doctor Mayo and Will toured many eastern hospitals for ideas.

The hospital is opened. — In 1889 the hospital was opened to all classes and denominations. There were thirteen patients at first. Both the sons assisted, working together as a team. Doctor Charles even made some of the instruments for the operating table. They operated only one or two mornings a week. The rest of the time was spent in visiting patients. The Sisters used lanterns to go about their duties at night.

The sons take over.—When Doctor Mayo turned seventy, he began to turn more and more work over to his sons, although people were sometimes skeptical about changing. Everyone had such faith in Doctor Mayo.

Mayo Clinic becomes famous.—As the practice grew, Mayo Clinic drew the best doctors in the world. More and more famous specialists were added to its staff. In 1915 the Mayo Clinic for Medical Education was formed. At the Mayo Clinic, outstanding young doctors who graduate from the University Medical School can take advanced work. People come from all over the world to be examined at the Mayo Clinic in Rochester.

Mayo Clinic.

St. Mary's Hospital.

CHAPTER THIRTY-SEVEN

James J. Hill
Empire Builder

When you hear of the Great Northern Railroad, you automatically think of James J. Hill. Destined to become the commanding and most constructive railroad genius of his age, he was born in a log cabin in Canada.

In 1856 he came to Minnesota. He found work as a shipping clerk for a river steamboat company in St. Paul. This was the beginning of his career in transportation. At that time he was a slender youth but he proved to be the fastest freight handler on the job.

Then and now.—If you ever take a ride across Minnesota on a train, think of when there were no railroads, the country was a wilderness and people traveled by ox cart or on horseback. The country was like that when Jim Hill came here but he was able to look ahead and see Minnesota

as a land of promise with homesteads and cabins and cities.

He meets his future wife.—While working in St. Paul, he met a waitress named Mary Teresa Mehegan. He fell in love with Mary but he wanted her to have a better education so he persuaded her to go to Milwaukee and enter a convent school.

Jim Hill forges ahead. — While Mary was getting educated, Jim Hill was getting ahead financially. He went into partnership with Norman Kittson who, you will recall, had a line of Red River carts carrying freight from Pembina to St. Paul. Before this, Jim explored the Red River country on snowshoes when it was 40 degrees below zero. In spite of the cold he realized this would some day be valuable territory.

Jim Hill rides to St. Anthony on

the William Crooks.—The first ten miles of railroad construction in Minnesota was from St. Paul to St. Anthony in 1862. The pioneer wood-burning locomotive had been brought up the river on a barge and was named the William Crooks. Jim Hill rode to St. Anthony on that first train.

Lives an active life.—In 1865 he entered the transportation field on his own account to represent a steamship line. This line of boats ran up and down the Red River.

The Civil War was in progress but he could not enlist because he had had

an accident which made him blind in one eye. So he raised a cavalry troop and sent them to war in his place.

In 1866 he became agent for the first division of the St. Paul and Pacific Railroad.

By 1868 he had a stock farm near St. Paul and raised only blooded stock.

By 1870 he had gone into a partnership which did general business in wood and coal and increased his business on the Red River.

Jim Hill set up and sold one of the first threshing machines in Minne-

im Hill rode on the William Crooks.

James J. Hill, "The Empire Builder."

sota. He got control of water power on the east side of the Falls of St. Anthony and became almost full owner of the St. Anthony Falls Waterpower.

He dreams of railroads. — He did all these things because he was constantly dreaming of railroads. He wanted to learn all about transportation and was quietly getting control of interests which would help him in railroading.

He realized that many companies had started short railroad lines and faced bankruptcy. By forming a company of wealthy men and assuming most of the control of the company, he was able to buy up these short lines. He combined them into a corporation called the "St. Paul, Minneapolis and Manitoba Railroad Company." Altogether they formed about

560 miles of completed road. That was not much when you compare it with present-day lines.

He was named general manager of the company, but by 1883 he was president. He rebuilt the old lines, improved grades and curves, changed the rails to steel and reduced freight rates.

All the time he kept thinking up ways to get his railroad used. He sent agents to Europe to persuade people to come to Minnesota to take up claims so the railroads could haul their grain. From brown paper, he cut the stencil for the label on the first barrel of flour milled for shipping from Minnesota. He got his tracks to the Red River and the Canadian border. Finally he built clear through to Seattle and it became the Great Northern.

Looking ahead. — Jim Hill was able to see far ahead. He bought up deposits of coal so as to have them when the need arose. He controlled iron mines. He found Oriental markets for his freight shipments. He persuaded farmers to use diversified methods and not plant the same crop year after year to wear out the soil. People everywhere looked up to him as a mental giant, though he was a short man with wrinkled skin and blind in one eye. One of his last remarks is often quoted. He said, "The railroad is in partnership with the land. It will prosper only as the land prospers."

He retired in 1912 and died four years later.

CHAPTER THIRTY-EIGHT

Jane Gray Swisshelm

*Editor . . . Abolitionist
Lecturer*

Although Jane Gray Swisshelm was a feminine sort of woman with blue eyes and a small mouth, she could show her claws like an angry little kitten when crossed.

In 1857 she came to St. Anthony from the East and brought her little daughter with her. At St. Anthony she took the stage to St. Cloud. On the stage she heard people discussing a man named Sylvanus B. Lowry. They said he lived in a big house with slaves from Tennessee to wait on him. They told how he kept an agent in Congress to pressure bills for him. They said he owned hundreds of acres of land. It sounded to her like Sylvanus B. Lowry was trying to run that part of Minnesota.

Jane starts a newspaper. — Jane went to live with her married sister but almost at once she started a newspaper. Being a strong-minded woman, she liked to get people stirred up by writing on controversial subjects. Remembering all she had heard about Sylvanus B. Lowry, she wrote fiery editorials attacking him for keeping slaves and trying to use pressure in Congress. She announced that St. Cloud was not big enough to hold both her and Mr. Lowry and that she did not intend to go.

Lowry fights back. — Mr. Lowry hired a man to give a lecture against women who dabbled in politics. She attended the lecture and took notes. Then she reported it in her paper and ridiculed Mr. Lowry at the same time. As a result, her office was broken into one night, wrecked, and part of the type thrown into the river.

Jane starts all over again.—Friends set her up again and she resumed publication. She wrote that anyone who reported a runaway slave would be tearing a man from his family and reducing him to the condition of a beast, outside the range of human sympathy. She could write bitterly about slavery but she showed the softer side of her nature when she wrote a series of columns called "Letters to Country Girls," where she gave advice on clothes and behaviour.

She becomes a lecturer.—She decided that she would become a lecturer in the fight against slavery and the cause of woman suffrage. Though she was a small woman with a soft voice, she gave such interesting talks that people thronged to hear her. She lectured on everything, including diet, child care, abolition and woman's rights. Once she was burned in effigy at St. Cloud and labeled "Mother of the Republican Party."

She made a tour of Minnesota, supporting abolition and women's rights. She rode in all sorts of conveyances, slept in all kinds of places, suffered ill health and kept right on. Often in winter she was almost frozen before she reached her destination.

Her political affiliations. — Jane Swisshelm was strong in praise of Lincoln and Fremont. But after the Indian massacres she got angry at Sibley because she thought he advocated too much leniency towards the culprits. Then she switched her support to Ignatius Donnelly.

Jane in the Civil War.—She went to Washington to help in the hospitals during the Civil War, but sent frequent articles back to Minnesota for publication. She was always pleading for lemons and other fruit to prevent scurvy in the hospitals.

St. Cloud Democrat Office

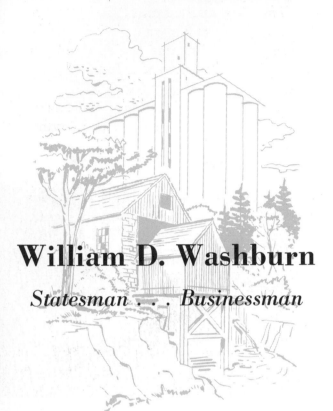

CHAPTER THIRTY-NINE

William D. Washburn

Statesman . . . Businessman

When William D. Washburn first came to Minneapolis, he set up a law office but was almost immediately appointed agent for the Minneapolis Mill Company. In this capacity, he saw something of the possibilities of making money in the fast-growing city.

He had already learned something about politics by working as a clerk in the House of Representatives while studying law in Washington.

In 1858 he became a member of the Minnesota State Legislature. He married the next year, and in 1861

he was commissioned by President Lincoln to serve as Surveyor General of Minnesota. His headquarters were in St. Paul. In this job he learned something of the wonderful timber possibilities in the state. At the close of his term, he returned to Minneapolis. He divided his career into three parts. They were business, statesmanship and promotion of public improvements.

He built a saw mill and went into lumbering. He started the St. Paul, Sault Ste. Marie railroad which carried produce to the east without going through Chicago. He built up the dam on the west side and this improved both lumbering and milling. He had one saw mill at Minneapolis and another at Anoka.

Feeling that wheat as well as lumber was the hope of the future, he built great mills on the west side. The

B mill was six stories high and faced the railroad tracks. It turned out 800 barrels a day and cost $100,000. In 1878 the A mill exploded from spontaneous combustion. The whole roof soared into the air and broke into bits. Fire broke out and burned everything. Fourteen men lost their lives and the loss might have run into hundreds if it had not occurred after working hours when only a maintenance crew were on hand.

After this he consolidated his interests with the Pillsbury's. This formed the largest flour milling corporation in the world.

Along with milling, Mr. Washburn was interested at all times in finance, real estate and railroads. His railroad penetrated 70 miles into Dakota. In 1888 he consolidated his east and west roads. While in the Legislature, he worked at getting flood control on the upper Mississippi.

During this time he had a big boat running on Lake Minnetonka called "The City of St. Louis." It could accommodate 600 passengers for pleasure rides. This was the first inland boat in the northwest to have electric lights. It ran eight years.

His home at "Fair Oaks" in Minneapolis was a social and cultural center.

A Washburn Mill.

Explosion at Mills.

CHAPTER FORTY

Ignatius Donnelly

Orator . . . Politician
Author

Three miles from Hastings is a ghost town where one of the stormiest figures in Minnesota once lived. He lived in a big house with little slits in the third story for defense against the Indians who never came there. He was Ignatius Donnelly. He came when he was twenty-six years old and started a town he called Ninninger.

His profession was law. His partner was John Ninninger, brother-in-law of Governor Ramsey. Donnelly laid out the town, dreaming that it would become a great city. He built a saw mill, a dance pavilion and a hotel. He subscribed $500 towards a steam ferry.

He pushed the town. — Using his eloquence to paint pictures, he literally talked the town into existence.

There were 3800 lots. The price of lots went up from five dollars to two hundred dollars. He started a newspaper called the "Emigrant Aid Journal of Minnesota." He circulated it all over the east and south, urging people to come to Ninninger. Some two hundred homes were built. He advocated a free library, school and lyceum. The town was boomed in newspapers, pamphlets and mass meetings. Because Donnelly was the leading figure at parties and dances, there were many exciting arguments. He had a round chubby face and hands, and was very expressive.

The bank failures of 1857 ruined his dreams. People moved to St. Paul, Hastings, or other places and he was left to farm at the site of a ghost town.

The deserted Donnelly Home.

He turns to politics.—Because he could not be restrained from using his brilliant mind, he turned to politics. He gave eloquent speeches. People loved to listen to him. However, he was a Republican one time, a Populist another and again he might claim some other affiliation. He was constantly in political hot water and he seemed to enjoy it. He was elected a lieutenant governor under Ramsey. Later, he was sent to Congress.

Donnelly as a writer. — When he failed to get a re-election for Congress, he turned to writing. One of his best known books was "Atlantis." It was the story of a fabulous island in the Pacific Ocean.

To this day he is known as the sage of Ninninger.

THE GREAT CRYPTOGRAM: FRANCIS BACON'S CIPHER in The SO-CALLED SHAKESPEARE PLAYS.

BY IGNATIUS DONNELLY, Author of "Atlantis: The Antediluvian World," and "Ragnarök: The Age of Fire and Gravel".

"And now I will vnclaspe a Secret booke
And to your quicke conceyuing Difcontents
Ile reade you Matter, deepe and dangerous,
As full of perill and aduenturous Spirit,
As to o'erwalke a Current, roaring loud,
On the vnftedfaft footing of a Speare."
1st Henry IV. Act I, Sc. 3.

·Chicago;
·New York and London·
R. S. Peale & Company.
1888.

CHAPTER FORTY-ONE

John S. Pillsbury

Father of University
Statesman

In 1853 many young men were coming to Minnesota to seek their fortunes but one came who was to make a lasting mark on the pages of history. That was John S. Pillsbury.

As a boy he had studied printing in New Hampshire but he had his eyes on a bigger future and went into a store to learn selling. When he got to the Falls of St. Anthony, he looked over the situation with an appraising eye. He had found a combination of water power, timber and transportation which could not help but mean growth.

He begins his career. — He began his career by opening a hardware store to supply the lumbermen who outfitted themselves and their men before going into the woods. His business flourished. He stretched his credit to the limit and had his warehouse filled with stock. He was elected to the city council because people realized he was a man to be looked up to.

The Panic of 1857. — People just couldn't believe the Panic of 1857 was really happening. Land values had been rising steadily. Immigrants had been pouring in, making for a steady increase in building and sales. Then almost overnight the Panic hit. Building stopped. People had no money with which to buy. John Pillsbury felt the pinch. People wanted to buy from him on credit yet he had no money to pay his creditors. On top of that a disastrous fire occurred and his warehouse and all its contents burned to the ground. He lost $38,000 worth of stock, most of it unpaid for.

He gave notes to all his creditors and went to work to pay off the notes, a few dollars at a time. For five years he and his wife denied themselves everything to pay those bills. Gradually he worked into the wholesale hardware business.

Organization of regiments.—When the Civil War started in 1861, he organized regiments to go to the front. When the Sioux massacres began he organized more regiments to protect the border. At the same time he was beginning to buy up pine lands.

Many activities.—In 1863 he was elected to the state senate. The same year he was made a regent of the University of Minnesota. The school was hopelessly in debt with mortgages totaling $100,000. The entire school was threatened with collapse.

Minnesota had public domain lands to establish colleges but no one seemed to want them. John Pillsbury proposed they create a special board with power to sell these lands and pay off the debts. He was made chairman of that board and in four years he had cleared the University of debt, often using his own money to meet pressing demands. His support of the University endeared him to the whole state.

While he worked for the University and in the Senate, some of his

Statue of Pillsbury at U. of M.

own investments in pine lands and other speculations had begun to pay off and he was becoming a wealthy man. In 1872 he realized that Minneapolis was slated to become the bread basket of the world if things were properly managed. He sent east for a nephew named Charles Pillsbury to go into milling with him. Together they invested $10,000 in a broken-down mill. Charles was to be manager at a salary of $1000 a year and a one-sixth interest of whatever he could make.

They got the old mill into working order. They bought wheat by the wagon load. It was not unusual for a

131

man to come to the mill with his wheat in a two-wheeled cart or in a sack on his back. They encouraged farmers to raise more and better wheat.

They installed a purifier to blow the bran from the wheat. This cleaned and graded the middlings but retained the wheat berry for grinding into flour. They let the bran run into the river.

The first year Charles, as manager, cleared $6000 as his share of the profits. "Pillsbury's Best Flour" was on the way to fame.

They hated to see all the bran running into the river because they felt it must have some commercial value. After some experimenting they developed a cattle food which became so popular they sold all the bran at a profit. After that, they installed steel rollers which improved flour grinding. Other members of the family came from the East to join in the business. John S. Pillsbury kept an interest but Charles was the manager and was very successful.

The mills had been operating about three years when John S. Pillsbury was elected governor without even running for office. He served three terms. Along with his milling interests, he became a director for the M & St. L. & Soo Line Railroad. He also served on directorates of several banks and the Stock Yards Co.

While he was governor, the state was ridden by the grasshopper plague.

In parts of the state, the very air quivered with their strange vibrations. The earth crawled with their shiny green bodies moving from field to garden. Farmers fought them, beating right and left but they were helpless against the millions of jaws working on corn and wheat. Many farmers were completely wiped out.

Governor Pillsbury went himself to visit those farms without letting people know who he was. He discovered their desperate needs. Often he left small gifts of money for temporary relief and once he took off his own overcoat and gave it to a farmer who couldn't get one for himself. All that winter he drove through the cold to learn the needs of the people. When he got back to St. Paul he set aside a day of prayer against the scourge. He got the legislature to assign funds for the needy. That winter the legislature paid for feeding and clothing 6000 people and the governor and his wife handled most of the details themselves.

Once while he was governor, a discussion came up in the legislature about the need of a science hall for the University. The Legislature did not feel they could allocate the necessary funds. Governor Pillsbury rose and quietly offered to give the University $150,000 for that purpose. After that he was known as the "Father of the University."

In the last years of his life, he gave more than a quarter of a million dollars to charitable institutions. In 1900 a statue of him was placed on the University campus. A gateway to the University has also been named in his honor.

Though John S. Pillsbury served in so many capacities, his big monument to the state is the University.

Scene at U. of M.

CHAPTER FORTY-TWO

Henry B. Whipple
Bishop

If you have gone through Faribault or lived there, you have no doubt seen Shattuck Military Academy and St. Mary's Hall. They are monuments to Bishop Henry Whipple. Few churchmen have left such a lasting impression on Minnesota as the Episcopal pastor, Bishop Whipple.

Served both Indians and Whites.—
Leaving a home of wealth and comfort, he came to Minnesota at a disastrous time just before the Civil War and the Sioux massacres. He served not only white parishioners but 17,000 redmen, most of them heathen. He traveled all over the state by canoe, stage and horseback to preach the simple Gospel of Jesus Christ.

Many of his parishes had been pre-viously organized by Rev. Doctor James Lloyd Breck, the first Episcopal missionary. While attending to those parishes, Bishop Whipple pushed his work among the Indians. He taught them, reconciled their quarrels, protected their interests, secured good treatment for them. He talked to them in camp and wigwam, making great efforts to influence them towards a pastoral life. He saw their good traits and said their temptations were developed by evil-minded white men. The Indians all loved and trusted Bishop Whipple. They called him "Straight Tongue."

Since there were few medical men or dentists, he learned to pull teeth and give simple remedies to relieve pain and illness. He founded a mission for the Indians on Cass Lake.

He gets lost.—Once, while driving from New Ulm to Fort Ridgley, he got lost in a snowstorm. He prayed for safety. Then he covered up with the buffalo robe and let the horses take their own course. They took him to the home of a missionary where he stayed until the storm was over.

He spoke out for the Indians.—He wrote letters and articles designed to mold public opinion. He labored with presidents and Federal authorities for Indian justice. He declared that the Indian Department was corrupt. He said not one treaty had been fairly carried out by the Government. In return the Indian agents denounced him for his defense of the Sioux, even after the massacres. He even dared to say the Government was responsible for the massacres because they had bungled the Indian payments.

He built a church. — In the dark hours of the Civil War, Bishop Whipple decided to build a church where young men could be trained for the ministry and teachers for schools. These were to be in Faribault where he made his headquarters.

A friend to the soldiers.—He was a friend to the soldiers enlisted in the Civil War. He held services for them at Fort Snelling. During the War he visited the army of the Potomac three times a year.

His schools. — On the site of the chapel where he held his first service

He visited Indian encampments.

are the two schools he founded, Shattuck Military Academy and St. Mary's Hall.

Church of St. Columba, Gull Lake.

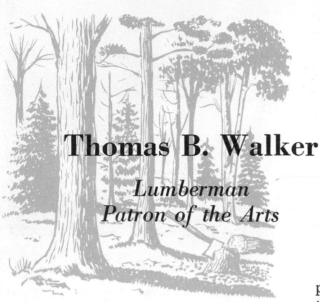

CHAPTER FORTY-THREE

Thomas B. Walker

*Lumberman
Patron of the Arts*

One of the outstanding buildings in Minneapolis is the Walker Art Center. This Center had its beginnings with the personal collections of a pioneer lumberman, Thomas Barlow Walker. Today it sponsors art and educational events for both adults and children. It exhibits outstanding collections of paintings, ceramics and jade.

Gray-eyed, young Thomas Walker came to St. Paul in 1862 when everyone was talking about the Indian massacres. He came upriver in a steamboat, bringing a load of grindstones which he had been trying to sell in every town from Chicago to St. Paul. He got rid of them in St. Paul and took the new ten-mile railroad, the first one in Minnesota, over to St. Anthony to find a job.

He finds work.—He got in with a party headed north to make surveys in the woods. They no sooner got started than the Indians north of St. Paul went on a rampage and the crew had to hurry to Fort Ripley near present Little Falls for protection. Returning to St. Paul, young Walker got a job examining land grants for a prospective railroad. This led to employment locating timber and he began to realize the possibilities of that industry in the new state.

Pleads for conservation.—Pine was becoming the way to wealth and power. The mills at St. Anthony cried out for lumber from every stream to the north. Men cut down trees with ruthlessness that was appalling. Walker began to preach conservation of our resources. At the time, no one listened. Today we have a State Department of Conservation formed to guard against depleting any of our natural resources.

Fort Ripley.

Starts his own company.—In 1877 he joined in a partnership with a Mr. Camp and they started their own lumbering business. The same year he pushed the idea of a Public Library in Minneapolis and was president of the first Library Board.

Starts an art collection.—He married and went with his wife to New York to buy furniture for their home. He bought a few pictures for their house. The next year he became so interested in collecting that he added some really important paintings. Then he built a gallery onto his home and the public was invited to come in at any time and see them.

He became interested in buying

Walker Art Center

pottery and jade. His jade collection became one of the finest in the world. He bought jewelry from old tombs and excavations. He had buyers in the Orient seeking out rare pieces.

His interests were wide. — His thoughts covered the heavens, nature, the whole range of literature and the world of man. Though he was a shrewd adventurer in business, he believed that a good character was the greatest asset any man could have.

Becomes a millionaire. — Through his mills at Crookston and Grand Forks called the Red River Lumber Company, and through other investments he became a millionaire. Yet his life always had the purpose of making money to help others. He founded several worth-while clubs, brought wholesale establishments to the city and started a public market where farmers could sell direct to consumers.

A monument to posterity.—Walker Art Institute is a monument to a great man. Today it encourages contemporary arts and local collectors. It draws thousands of visitors to its exhibitions and special events.

Log Jam.

CHAPTER FORTY-FOUR

Merritt Brothers

Miners

Have you ever ridden through northern Minnesota and seen the great iron mines on the Vermillion, Mesabi and Cuyuna Ranges? The Mesabi means giant and is the largest, stretching across Itasca and St. Louis Counties for a hundred miles. The city of Brainerd is the southern gateway to these deep, open pit mines known as the Cuyuna Mountain Range and Chisholm is in the heart of the Mesabis. Ely, on the Vermillion range, has four iron mines right inside the city.

The man with seven sons.—In 1863 when Lewis and Hepsibeth Merritt came to Duluth with their seven sons they lived at Conner's Point where Lewis had a saw mill. After treaties opened up the country, Lewis took squatter's rights to a tract of land in west Duluth on the St. Louis River.

Lewis believed there was iron in the Mesabi Range and he got all his seven sons fired with the idea. At first Jerome taught school. Leonidas joined up with Sibley and helped drive the warring Sioux out of Minnesota. Albert and Andrew built boats. Cassius helped out all around and the two youngest hadn't started working yet. All of them took up claims as soon as they were old enough but they weren't farmers. They could think nothing but iron.

Searching the hills.—At that time few white men went into the trackless white pine forests and swampy land which covered the north country. The Merritts went although people thought they were crazy. Even while Leonidas was off with Sibley,

139

the other brothers kept right on searching the hills north of Duluth.

Dressed in heavy mackinaws and cowhide boots, they walked the Vermillion Trail through swamps and forests, performing heroic feats of endurance. Sometimes they used the canoe route down the north shore of Lake Superior to Pigeon Point or Grand Portage and then walked from there.

They traveled under great difficulty. — They carried everything on their backs and the loads were heavy. Each man needed two blankets, a small tent, simple medicines, hatchet, dishes for cooking and eating, and essential foods, besides compass, gun and fishing tackle. They fought mosquitoes, cleared trails, and found shelter from storms. They had to make their way through uncharted country. They had to understand the geology of the country.

Sometimes they could use a dog team. Occasionally they were able to use a lumber wagon though the wheels sank deep in pine needles or got bogged in red, powdery soil.

Cassius finds new evidence. — In 1887 Cassius went exploring with a crew for a railroad company who wanted to run a line from Duluth to Winnipeg. He came back with some samples of iron ore he had found. This spurred them on.

They buy up claims.—In 1889 they went south from Tower to look for ore. Before going there, they bought

They walked through dense woods seeking iron.

up one year prospecting leases for $25.00 each. Leonidas took out 114 leases and they explored towards Iron Mountain. If they found ore, they could get leases to mine for fifty years by paying $100 and a royalty of 25 cents a ton on all the iron they took out.

Iron is discovered.—Men in their crew actually found the first iron. It lay in a shallow basin and there was acres and acres of it. The Merritts began to exploit their find.

They needed a railroad.—The Merritts knew they had to have a railroad to get the iron out. They ran a branch line to Superior to where there was already a railroad and over it they shipped the first cargo of ore.

They go into business. — Shedding boots and mackinaws, one of the boys opened a store at Iron Mountain just south of Virginia. Another one started a bank. Nearby Virginia sprang to life only to be wiped out by a fire that forced them to start building all over again.

Financial difficulties.— There was a temporary depression and the Merritts faced bankruptcy. They borrowed money from John D. Rockefeller to extend the railroad and continue their other interests. They did not understand Big Business at all. They took out new mortgages to pay old ones. Suddenly it was no longer the Merritt business at all. Everything had been taken over by foreclosures.

The mines are their monument.— Though they do not bear the Merritt name, the mines in northern Minnesota are monuments to a family of brothers who refused to give up. Minnesota iron is famous throughout the world.

Open Pit Mine near Hibbing.

143

CHAPTER FORTY-FIVE

John Ireland

Archbishop

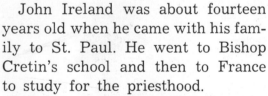

John Ireland was about fourteen years old when he came with his family to St. Paul. He went to Bishop Cretin's school and then to France to study for the priesthood.

He returned to St. Paul a tall rugged young man with sharp intellectual features and a bright face. He was ordained and assigned as a chaplain for the Fifth Minnesota Regiment in the Civil War. He went south with the troops but when they got to Vicksburg he contracted a serious fever and was returned to Minnesota. He was made a secretary to the Bishop but soon had his own pastorate.

He takes strong stands. — Going about St. Paul in long frock coat, slouch hat and old boots, he became known for his good works. He was noticed for his oratory also and he used this gift to take a firm stand for temperance. Many times he painted vivid word pictures of ruined homes, poverty and unhappiness, caused by drinking alcoholic beverages.

His promotions.—By 1875 he was a coadjustor bishop and worked to get aid for Indian schools. He took a very active part in civic affairs, backing law enforcement leagues to the limit.

In 1884 he was a Bishop and helped found St. Thomas College. He urged

Catholics to build churches, schools and seminars.

He starts colonies. — He worked with Jim Hill to bring immigrants to Minnesota. He pleaded for colonists who could succeed in western agriculture but imposed no restrictions about religious or social status. He helped start colonies at Graceville, Clontarf, De Graff, Ghent, Currie, Avoca, Iona, Fulda and Adrian.

In 1888 he became Archbishop and his influence was then national. He was in close alliance with almost every president of his time. He saw St. Paul grow from a thousand population to a quarter million.

His last great efforts were in connection with the erection of the magnificent St. Paul Cathedral and the beautiful Basilica of St. Mary's in Minneapolis.

St. Paul Cathedral.

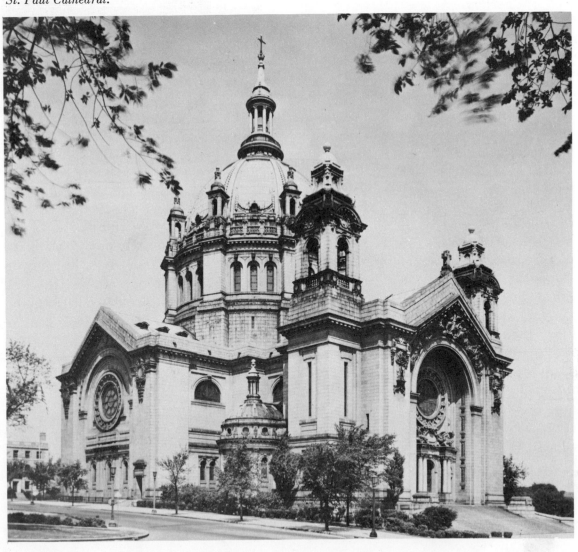

143

Credit
Minnesota Historcial Society
Minneapolis Public Library
Minnesota Division of Publicity
Great Northern Railroad
United States Forest Service
Pillsbury Milling Company
Riehle Studios
Minnesota Department of Business Development